Abiding in Christ

Abiding in Christ

by
John MacArthur, Jr.

WORD OF GRACE COMMUNICATIONS
P.O. Box 4000
Panorama City, CA 91412

All Scripture quotations, unless noted otherwise, are from the *New Scofield Reference Bible*, King James Version. Copyright © 1967 by Oxford University Press, Inc. Reprinted by permission.

Scripture quotations marked NASB are from the *New American Standard Bible*, © 1960, 1962, 1963, 1968, 1971, 1972, 1973, 1975, and 1977 by The Lockman Foundation, and are used by permission.

Library of Congress Cataloging in Publication Data

MacArthur, John F.
    Abiding in Christ.

    (John MacArthur's Bible studies)
    Includes index.
    1. Bible. N.T. John XV, 1-25—Criticism, interpretation, etc. I. Title. II. Series: MacArthur, John F. Bible studies.
BS2615.2.M275   1986   226'.506   86-12767
ISBN 0-8024-5128-4 (pbk.)

1 2 3 4 5 6 7 Printing/GB/Year 91 90 89 88 87 86

Printed in the United States of America

Contents

These Bible studies are taken from messages delivered by Pastor-Teacher John MacArthur, Jr., at Grace Community Church in Panorama City, California. These messages have been combined into a 6-tape album entitled *Abiding in Christ*. You may purchase this series either in an attractive vinyl cassette album or as individual cassettes. To purchase these tapes, request the album *Abiding in Christ* or ask for the tapes by their individual GC numbers. Please consult the current price list; then, send your order, making your check payable to:

WORD OF GRACE COMMUNICATIONS
P.O. Box 4000
Panorama City, CA 91412

Or, call the following toll-free number:
1-800-55-GRACE

1

The Vine and the Branches

Introduction

The fifteenth chapter of John is one of the most important chapters in the Bible. However, at the same time it is a difficult chapter to understand because of interpretive problems. This classic chapter contains a meaningful allegory—one of the great "I am" passages recorded by John that points to the deity of Jesus Christ. The foundational principles for living the Christian life—abiding in Christ and bearing fruit—are recorded in this chapter and elucidated in the New Testament epistles.

A. Presenting the Problem

We're going to begin with a basic interpretation of the various features of this allegory of a vine, its branches, and the vinedresser—the one who cares for the vine. The key to the passage is the identification of the branches. There are two groups of branches in the passage: ones that bear fruit (vv. 2, 8) and ones that do not (vv. 2, 6). The branches that bear fruit are Christians. The branches that do not bear fruit are not so easily identified. Are they Christians or non-Christians? If they are Christians, why are they thrown into the fire and burned? Does that mean Christians can lose their salvation and perish or that they are chastised for not bearing fruit? I believe the Word of God clearly identifies the fruitless branches.

B. Setting the Scene

1. The context

The events recorded in John 15 take place on the night before the death of Jesus while He is speaking with His disciples. The context of the passage might cause us to wonder why Jesus used this allegory. I believe the thoughts of Jesus on that night involved what was happening among the disciples. The fourteenth chapter records that Christ spent His time comforting His disciples before His arrest and crucifixion. He knew He was going to be separated from the Father when He died the next day. Jesus also was aware that Judas, who had already been dismissed from the room, was plotting His betrayal. Jesus was thinking about all the characters involved in that final night: the eleven disciples, the Father who loved Him, and Judas—who did not. Consequently, I believe that the key to understanding the allegory in John 15 is related to the characters in the drama. Since Jesus claimed to be the Vine and identified the Vinedresser as the Father, it is reasonable to conclude that the branches that bear fruit would be the eleven true disciples, and the branches that do not bear fruit refer to Judas and any others who were never true disciples.

2. The cleansing

In John 13:10 Jesus says, "He that is washed needeth not except to wash his feet." Once you've been spiritually cleansed, or saved, you need only a little foot-washing periodically—a reference to the continuing forgiveness of God. You don't need to take the major bath of salvation again. Jesus then told His disciples, "Ye are clean, but not all of you. For he knew who should betray him; therefore said he, Ye are not all clean" (vv. 10-11). Jesus was well aware of a distinction among His own disciples regarding their salvation: the contrast between Judas and the eleven. I believe that contrast is carried into the fifteenth chapter, where Jesus talks about the two kinds of branches. All the disciples had contact with Jesus for roughly the same amount of time. Although Judas appeared to be a believer and even had the privileged responsibility of maintaining the funds for the disciples, he was a branch that never bore fruit. God finally removed him from the Vine to experience the eternal burning of hell.

3. The controversy

Some people would conclude that Judas lost his salvation and that if any Christian fails to bear fruit he also will lose his salvation. However, John 10:28 says, "I give unto them eternal life; and they shall never perish, neither shall any man pluck them out of my hand." The Word of God is absolutely clear about the security of salvation. In John 6:37 Jesus says, "All that the Father giveth me shall come to me." In chapter 17 He tells the Father, "Those that thou gavest me I have kept, and none of them is lost, but the son of perdition" (v. 12). Those statements reveal that Jesus was not talking about a true believer who stops bearing fruit and loses his salvation. Rather, He was talking about a Judas-type believer, who is superficially attached to the vine but never receives spiritual nourishment from it. Judas had a superficial relationship with Jesus, but he willingly walked away from that relationship and into the judicial condemnation of God. It seems natural that the allegory of the vine and the branches would come out of Christ's intimate talk with the eleven disciples who believed in Him.

4. The contrast

In the upper room, Jesus talked with the disciples about branches that do not bear fruit and are taken away and burned—referring to men like Judas. There are people today who similarly stand in close connection with Jesus Christ but are apostates and doomed to hell. They may attend church and go through some religious exercises, thinking that their superficial connection to Him is sufficient for salvation, but they are not legitimate believers. On the other hand, the eleven disciples and all who truly abide in Christ show the reality of their faith by the fruit they bear. The contrast between true and false disciples is common in the gospel of John.

Lesson

I. THE VINE (v. 1a)

"I am the true vine."

In speaking to the eleven remaining disciples in the upper room, Jesus chose the metaphor of a vine because of its manifold significance. A vine planted in the ground speaks of the humility of One who came in the form of a man, planted in the earth, so to speak. The figure of a vine pictures an intimate union with branches that are totally dependent upon it. A vine is a classic illustration for showing fruit-bearing as evidence of spiritual productivity.

A. Its Illustration in the Old Testament

Israel was identified as God's vine in the Old Testament. God was "the husbandman" (John 15:1, KJV*) who operated through His people. He cared for Israel, cutting off branches that were not bearing fruit. Although faith was necessary for salvation, just being Jewish brought great blessing. Isaiah 5:1-7 illustrates that: "Now will I sing to my well-beloved [God] a song of my beloved touching his vineyard [Israel]. My well-beloved hath a vineyard in a very fruitful hill. And he dug it, and gathered out the stones, and planted it with the choicest vine, and built a tower in the midst of it, and also made a winepress in it; and he looked for it to bring forth grapes, and it brought forth wild grapes. And now, O inhabitants of Jerusalem, and men of Judah, judge, I pray you, between me and my vineyard. What could have been done more to my vineyard, that I have not done in it? Why, when I looked for it to bring forth grapes, brought it forth wild grapes? And now, I tell you what I will do to my vineyard: I will take away its hedge, and it shall be eaten up; break down its wall, and it shall be trampled down. And I will lay it waste; it shall not be pruned, nor digged, but there shall come up briers and thorns; I will also command the clouds that they rain no rain upon it. For the vineyard of the Lord of hosts is the house of Israel." Israel forfeited God's blessing by failing to bear fruit. The nation experienced God's judgment by being taken captive for having failed to bear fruit.

The vine became so much a symbol of Israel that it appeared on coins minted during the Maccabean period, which was between the Old and New Testaments. During the time of Christ, Herod's Temple had a vine on it overlaid with gold that some have estimated was worth $12 million. Israel had always been God's vine, but it had become unproductive, so a new vine was established.

B. Its Realization in the New Testament

No longer would a man receive blessing through a covenant relationship to Israel but through the new Vine, who is Christ. With the coming of the New Covenant established by Christ, a man would have to be intimately connected to Jesus Christ to receive spiritual life and bear fruit.

*King James Version.

The word "true" (Gk., *alēthinos*) is used here in the sense of "eternal," "heavenly," or "divine," a common usage in Scripture. (That means Christ is the perfect heavenly reality of which Israel was a prophetic picture in the Old Testament.) Israel was a type of God's messianic servant, and Jesus Christ was the fulfillment (Isa. 41:8-9; 53:11). Hebrews 8:2 speaks of "the true tabernacle, which the Lord pitched, and not man," showing the contrast between an earthly picture and the spiritual reality. The Lord has planted Christ as the perfect Vine. All that could possibly be symbolized in a vine comes to fulfillment in Christ. Perhaps that is why Paul says in Colossians 2:7 that Christians are "rooted and built up in him."

Christ is the true Vine in the sense that He is "the true Light" (John 1:9). There have been many times when God revealed His truth before, but Christ is its perfect revelation. All that could be conceived in the concept of spiritual light is realized in Christ. He is the highest essence of spiritual light, as opposed to physical light and to believers, who are lights in the world (Matt. 5:14). Similarly, Jesus called Himself the "bread of life" (John 6:35). The Israelites were physically sustained by the manna in the desert (v. 31), a type of Christ. So all that the metaphor of a vine could possibly claim of spiritual value is true of Jesus Christ.

What Is Your Vine?

It's amazing how many people who claim to be Christians have other vines in their lives from which they seek their resources. I have tried to determine if there are any other vines than Christ in my life. Ask yourself, "How many things do I attach myself to for my well-being? Some people think their vine is their bank account, education, sexual relationships, popularity, skills, connections, possessions, or social relationships. Some people even think the church is their vine. They attach themselves to a system of religion. But their vine should be Jesus Christ, not the church. Attending a church is not necessarily evidence of a vine-branch relationship. In fact, it can be a parasitic relationship—sometimes people are like parasites because they attend church only for what it will do for them. You as a

10

branch must grow with Christ as your Vine. Not even a Bi-
ble-study group or a church can be a substitute for Jesus
Christ as your sustenance for living.

Israel was the vine of the Old Testament, but Christ is the Vine
in the New Testament. Israel, however, was usually referred to
as a degenerate vine. By marvelous contrast, Jesus Christ is
"the same yesterday, and today, and forever" (Heb. 13:8). He
is a Vine that will never wither—the kind of vine I want to be
attached to.

II. THE VINEDRESSER (v. 1*b*)

"My Father is the vinedresser."

A. The Analogy of a Farmer

The vinedresser was the one who cared for the vines in a
vineyard. As a farmer, he was responsible to cut off the
branches that bore no fruit because they tended to sap the
energy from the fruit-bearing branches. That increased the
productivity of the other branches. The vinedresser also
constantly pruned the branches that could bear fruit to enable the vine to concentrate its energy on maturing so that
it could bear more fruit. Verse 2 says the Father as the
Vinedresser purges the vine "that it may bring forth more
fruit." Verse 8 tells us He wants the branches to "bear
much fruit." The one who cared for the vine chopped off the
branches that bore no fruit and threw them away. The
vine's soft wood made them useless. Therefore, the
branches of the vine were thrown away and consumed in a
bonfire.

B. The Application to the Father

1. His work of punishing

The Father "taketh away" the branches that fail to bear
fruit. Verse 2 doesn't say He fixes them up; it says He
cuts them off. Verse 6 says that those branches are gathered, thrown into a pile, and burned. The Father deals
with them with finality. Now if that refers to a Christian, we've got some problems. I believe that the fruit-

less branches refer to people who profess to have a relationship to Jesus Christ—who apparently are in the Vine as followers of Christ—but are like Judas and have never been saved. That is obvious because they never bear spiritual fruit. At a certain point in the Father's timing, the fruitless branches are cut off for the life and health of the Vine and the other branches. Professing Christians who aren't really saved and therefore don't bear fruit will be cast away and burned in an act of divine punishment.

2. His work of pruning

The second work of the Father in verse 2 is to purge "every branch that beareth fruit." That phrase refers to the true Christian. The Father has some work to do on Christians also. But it's not a final work; it's the continuing work of purging. The word *purge* means "to cleanse" or "to prune" in the context of the allegory of a vine. The Father purges or prunes a branch that bears fruit (a Christian) so that it might bear more fruit (become spiritually mature).

III. THE VINE BRANCHES (vv. 2-3)

The branches on the vine grow rapidly. They must be tended carefully, which requires drastic pruning on a regular basis. To have a fruitful vine, a vinedresser must cut off the fruitless branches for the sake of the vine's health and productivity. He must also carefully prune away all the shoots and other things that gather on the fruit-bearing branches that tend to sap the strength of the vine. Jesus said that some of His followers are like branches who bear fruit but need to be pruned. Others are like branches that don't bear fruit and are ultimately eliminated by being cast into a fire.

A. The Professing Branches (v. 2a)

"Every branch in me that beareth not fruit he taketh away."

1. The lacking requirement

I believe a fruitless branch cannot represent a Christian

because there is fruit in every Christian's life. With some Christians you've got to look a long time, but there will be fruit in their lives. The essence of new life in Christ is its productivity.

a) Ephesians 2:10—"We are his workmanship, created in Christ Jesus unto good works, which God hath before ordained that we should walk in them." The fruit of salvation is good works.

b) James 2:17, 22—"Even so faith, if it hath not works, is dead" (v. 17). A life that has no evidence of fruitful works does not have an active faith. Legitimate saving faith is productive, even if it's only in a minimal sense. Verse 22 says, "Seest thou how faith wrought with [Abraham's] works, and by works was faith made perfect?" That doesn't mean you're saved by works; it means your works are the end product or evidence of salvation.

c) Matthew 7:16-17, 20—"Ye shall know them by their fruits. Do men gather grapes of thorns, or figs of thistles? Even so, every good tree bringeth forth good fruit. . . . Wherefore, by their fruits ye shall know them." The attitudes and actions of a person reveal whether an individual is a believer or not. There is no such thing as a believer who doesn't bring forth good fruit.

d) Matthew 12:33—"Either make the tree good, and its fruit good, or else make the tree corrupt, and its fruit corrupt; for the tree is known by its fruit."

e) Matthew 3:7-8—"When [John the Baptist] saw many of the Pharisees and Sadducees come to his baptism, he said unto them, O generation of vipers, who hath warned you to flee from the wrath to come? Bring forth, therefore, fruits befitting repentance"—that is, fruits that are connected with salvation.

f) Romans 6:20-22—"When ye were the servants of sin, ye were free from righteousness. What fruit had ye then in those things of which ye are now ashamed?" (v. 21). The implied answer is none, because they weren't saved. Any fruit they had was the fruit of sin. The contrast comes in verse 22: "But now being made free from sin, and become servants to God, ye have your fruit unto holiness, and the end everlasting life." Every believer has everlasting life, which is the culmination of a righteous life. Therefore people who don't bear fruit cannot be believers.

2. The limited relationship

There are two words in verse 2 that seem to contradict what I've just said: "in me." That sounds like the people who don't bear fruit are Christians because of their association with Christ. But I don't think they are, and a few scriptural illustrations will show why.

a) Luke 8:18—"Take heed, therefore, how ye hear; for whosoever hath, to him shall be given; and whosoever hath not, from him shall be taken even that which he seemeth to have." Some relationships to Christ are in appearance only.

b) Romans 11:20—Paul pictured Israel as an olive tree. However some of the branches of that tree weren't saved. God broke off the branches that weren't connected to the tree and deriving their life from it. Verse 20 says, "Because of unbelief they were broken off." The branches in John 15 present the same analogy.

c) 1 John 2:19—"They went out from us, but they were not of us; for if they had been of us, they would no doubt have continued with us; but they went out, that they might be made manifest that they were not all of us." An individual can apparently seem connected to Jesus Christ but, in fact, not be connected at all.

The apostle Paul warns against being superficially attached to Christ. If you come to church merely out of a superficial allegiance to Jesus Christ, heed Paul's warning: "Examine yourselves, whether you are in the faith; prove yourselves. Know ye not yourselves how Jesus Christ is in you, unless you are discredited?" (2 Cor.

14

13:5). He exhorts us to check our lives to make sure our salvation is real. It's a stern warning.

Were the Branches to Be Burned Once Believers?

Jesus is talking about two kinds of branches: the branches that are true disciples and the Judas branches—ones that hang around Him with a facade of faith. The latter appear to believe because they are superficially attached. When the Father removes them, they are never able to come back. People who say the branches that are burned refer to Christians put themselves in a very difficult position. The burning of the branches would seem to imply that if you lost your salvation, you could never get it back again. People who believe that support it with Hebrews 6:6, which says it's impossible "to renew [those who have fallen away] again unto repentance." However, people who hold to such a position often think they can be saved more than once. But according to every passage that talks about falling away, there is no chance to come back in faith. Actually, those passages refer to apostates, who superficially attach themselves to Christ yet were never genuine believers to begin with.

B. The Possessing Branches (vv. 2b-3)

1. The intention of pruning (v. 2b)

"Every branch that beareth fruit, he purgeth it, that it may bring forth more fruit."

Every believer in Christ gets purged because "whom the Lord loveth he chasteneth, and scourgeth every son whom he receiveth" (Heb. 12:6). If you can look at your problems as a divine procedure for becoming more fruitful, you might even be tempted to pray for trouble! The Greek word translated "purgeth" (*kathairō*) means "to clean." Although it is used in only one other place in the New Testament, extrabiblical Greek literature uses it to refer to cleansing grain (separating it from the waste material) and cleansing the soil of weeds before planting a crop. Using that word, the first-century Jewish philosopher Philo said the superfluous shoots that grow on plants are a great injury to the genuine shoots, which the vinedresser cleanses (*kathairō*) by pruning.

In the case of spiritual pruning, the Father removes things like sin or worldly distractions that would hinder our fruit-bearing, because He wants us to operate at maximum capacity. Suffering is one of the best methods of purging. It has a way of cleaning out the life whose growth has been stunted. Although spiritual pruning can be painful and may not seem to be necessary from our perspective, the Father knows what He is doing. His valuable lessons of suffering can identify what is not necessary in our lives and needs to be removed. The Father's pruning may take the form of sickness, hardship, loss of material goods, slander and persecution, loss of loved ones, grief in relationships, or war. God ordained troubles to prune the things in our lives that drain away our energy and rob us of our capacity to bear fruit. But it is wonderful to know that the Father cares that we bear much fruit. Don't think God is up in heaven snapping a big whip and saying, "Bear fruit, or I'll get you!" He is carefully helping us to bear fruit. Aren't you glad that God is involved in your life for that purpose? Do you look at your trials like that, or do you lapse into self-pity, fear, or complaining? But if you realize that God desires to increase your productivity, then the pruning process can be a joyful experience.

Hebrews 12 says, "If ye endure chastening, God dealeth with you as with sons; for what son is he whom the father chasteneth not? . . . For they verily for a few days chastened us after their own pleasure, but he for our profit, that we might be partakers of his holiness" (vv. 7, 10). We are purged by God that we might partake of His holiness. The divine pruning knife may hurt a bit, but it is worth it.

2. The instrument of pruning (v. 3)

"Now ye are clean through the word which I have spoken unto you."

What is the Father's knife? Although He may use things

16

such as suffering in the purging process, I think the divine pruning instrument is the Word of God. Jesus told the disciples that they were spiritually purged, or cleansed, through "the word." Affliction is only the handle of the knife where God gets His grip. Have you ever noticed how much more sensitive you are to the Word of God when you're in trouble? The Spirit of God applies Scripture to your heart in adversity. Trouble opens our eyes to receive the divine surgery performed by the Word. A trial puts pressure on us and helps us to develop spiritual muscles, but the Word is "the two-edged sword" that does the cutting (Heb. 4:12). Charles Spurgeon, the great nineteenth-century English preacher, said: "It is the Word that prunes the Christian, it is the truth that purges him, the Scripture made living and powerful by the Holy Spirit—effectually cleanses the Christian. Affliction is the handle of the knife—affliction is the grindstone that sharpens the Word—affliction is the dresser that removes our soft garments and lays bear the diseased flesh, so that the surgeon's knife may get at it—affliction merely makes us ready to feel the Word—but the true pruner is the Word, in the hand of the Great Vinedresser."

When Jesus told the disciples that they had been cleansed through the Word, He was indicating that their initial salvation came through the Word. Similarly, their continual pruning would be done by the Word as well. When you're being afflicted, you focus more on the Word and see how it applies to you. As you experience affliction, the Word cuts away hindrances to your spiritual growth.

Are you aware of the Father's purpose in pruning you? Do you know what's going on in your life when you have trouble? God's purpose in pruning is so you will bear more fruit. Are you a fruit-bearing branch—a real believer? Or are you superficially just hanging on to Christ? If so, you're in danger of hell because some day the Father will remove you. I hope you know your only source of life is the true Vine, which is Jesus Christ.

1. What two foundational principles for living the Christian life are recorded in John 15 (see p. 6)?
2. In the allegory of the vine and its branches, who are the branches that bear fruit (see p. 6)?
3. Describe the scene during which John 15 takes place (see pp. 6-7).
4. Explain how the context of John 15 is the key to understanding the allegory of the vine and the branches (see p. 7).
5. According to John 13:10-11, what type of cleansing does a Christian need once he's been saved? In what sense were eleven of the disciples clean (see p. 7)?
6. What verses reveal that the eleven true disciples could not lose their salvation (see pp. 7-8)?
7. What is a common contrast in the gospel of John (see p. 8)?
8. Identify God's vine in the Old Testament (see p. 9).
9. How did Israel forfeit God's blessing? What did the nation experience as a result (see p. 9)?
10. Rather than through a covenant relationship to Israel, how does a person receive a blessing under the New Testament (see pp. 9-10)?
11. What was the vinedresser responsible to do? Why (see p. 11)?
12. Who are the fruitless branches in the allegory of the vine (see pp. 11-12)?
13. Differentiate between the Father's works of punishing and pruning the branches (see pp. 11-12).
14. Why can't a fruitless branch represent a Christian? Support your answer with Scripture (see pp. 12-13).
15. In what sense are the fruitless branches "in" Christ (John 15:2; see p. 14)?
16. How did the people mentioned in 1 John 2:19 reveal they were not Christians to begin with (see p. 14)?
17. What is one of the Father's most effective ways of cleaning out the life of a person whose spiritual growth has been stunted? What are some of the forms that the Father's pruning may take (see p. 16)?
18. Why does the Father chasten us, according to Hebrews 12:10 (see p. 16)?
19. What is the divine pruning instrument (John 15:3; see pp. 16-17)?

Pondering the Principles

1. Although Christ is the Christian's only source of sufficiency, many believers have substituted other things for the true Vine. Since you've become a Christian, have you gravitated toward trusting more in your education, career, abilities, relationships, popularity, bank account, or possessions than in the Lord? Although most of those things are important, our security needs to be in the Lord. Read Luke 12:13-34, 2 Corinthians 12:7-10, and Philippians 4:10-19. As you evaluate your life in light of those verses, determine if you would still be content should any of the things that you have placed too much value on be taken away. When God allowed Job to lose his wealth and his sons, he replied, "Naked came I out of my mother's womb, and naked shall I return there. The Lord gave, and the Lord hath taken away; blessed be the name of the Lord" (Job 1:21). Pray that you might reflect Job's proper perspective when a loss occurs in your life. Although you might experience sadness because of the loss, an undergirding of trust in the sufficiency of the Lord will carry you through.

2. Are you sensitive to what the Holy Spirit is doing in your life through discipline or suffering? Are you in regular communication with the Father by praying to Him and reading His Word so that you can grow spiritually as you are being pruned? Thank God that though His purposes may cause us to experience pain, He is mindful of our frailty (Ps. 103:14) and seeks to make us bear more fruit (John 15:3, 6).

2

Abiding in the Vine—Part 1

Outline

Introduction

Lesson
I. The Basic Meaning of Abiding (vv. 4, 8-10)
   A. The Exhortation for the Unbeliever
      1. The plea (v. 4a)
         a) Explained
         b) Exhorted
            (1) Luke 8:14
            (2) 1 John 2:19
            (3) 1 John 2:24
            (4) Colossians 1:21-23
            (5) Hebrews 3:6, 14
            (6) Hebrews 4:14
      2. The promise (v. 4b)
      3. The parallels (vv. 8-10)
         a) Fruitfulness
         b) Love
         c) Obedience
   B. The Expectation for the Believer
      1. The ideal pattern
         a) Desiring eternal life
         b) Confessing sin
         c) Obeying God
         d) Loving Christians
         e) Not loving the world
         f) Not sinning
      2. The realistic perspective
         a) The failure
         b) The feeding
         c) The focus
            (1) Explained
            (2) Expressed

21

(*a*) Galatians 2:20
(*b*) Philippians 2:13
(*c*) Galatians 3:3

Introduction

There is a question that plagues more Christians than perhaps any other, and it is this: What is involved in having a vital relationship with Jesus Christ? Not only is it asked by believers in moments of sinfulness, discouragement, or confusion, but it is asked by unbelievers as well. How can we describe the union that a believer experiences between himself and Christ? We talk about knowing Christ, being in Christ, walking with Christ, and loving Christ. But what does that union really involve? It's like the relationship of two people in love, like the relationship between a father and his son, where there's mutual love and respect. Or it could be likened to the relationship between two close friends or between two brothers who would defend each other to the death. Perhaps the most graphic illustration of a believer's relationship to Christ is that of a vine and branches, given by our Lord Himself in John 15.

There are many truths in the allegory of the vine and the branches that give us insight into the Christian life. Our growth together with Christ is perfectly illustrated by a vine and a branch. We are nothing in ourselves; we gather all our strength from Him—our lives are filled with His energy and resources. By ourselves we can't produce fruit; we must be vitally connected to Christ, who produces fruit through us. In the beginning of John 15, Jesus uses that allegory to teach His disciples about a believer's relationship with Him and the Father. He also explains that the person who only appears to be connected to Him is not a legitimate believer and therefore will be cut off, thrown away, and burned.

In the last chapter, we met the Vine (Jesus Christ), the Vinedresser (the Father), and the two kinds of branches (the believers who bear fruit and the nonbelievers who don't). Jesus continues the analogy in verse 4 by making a heart-stirring plea: "Abide in me." He envisions people who are superficially attached to Him—people who may go to church, claim to be devout, and even talk about their relationship to Him—but who

22

aren't real believers. He exhorts the unbelieving fruitless branch to remain in Him. Jesus wants His superficial followers to become true believers, showing the legitimacy of their faith by remaining in Him. That is not to say a believer must work to stay saved, but that he will remain in Christ because he is a believer. To those who don't remain in Him, He gives a solemn warning in verse 6: "If a man abide not in me, he is cast forth as a branch." If a person who is apparently attached to Christ suddenly departs from the faith, it is natural to wonder what happened. The answer is simple: Such people were never true believers to begin with, otherwise they never would have left. The false branch does not remain with Christ.

Lesson

I. THE BASIC MEANING OF ABIDING (vv. 4, 8-10)

A. The Exhortation for the Unbeliever

1. The plea (v. 4a)

a) Explained

In verse 4, Jesus is saying to men like Judas, "Don't be superficial; be for real. Abide in Me and prove that your faith is real. You superficial branches need to be saved!" It's tragic when men superficially line up with Jesus Christ but never become true Christians. There are some believing wives who bring their unsaved husbands to church. They may appear to be Christians, but they really aren't. Sometimes young people come to church only because they want to be involved in a youth program, but they don't know Jesus Christ as Lord. Jesus calls to all who have made a statement of faith or an apparent identification with Him to be sure they're genuine believers.

Jesus says in verse 4, "Abide in me, and I in you. As the branch cannot bear fruit of itself, except it abide in the vine, no more can ye, except ye abide in me." The word "abide" simply means "to remain." Jesus is saying, "Be for real, and give evidence that you're

23

for real by remaining with Me." It's not that remaining in Christ saves you—that would be ridiculous because it would base your salvation on your ability to hang in there. Remaining in Christ is the evidence that you are saved. People often know someone who used to be involved in various church functions but all of a sudden disappeared and has never returned. That individual proved he was not a true believer because he didn't abide in Christ. He never was real to begin with. If a man really knows Jesus Christ, it is the character of the salvation experience for that man to remain in Christ. The false will always leave sooner or later.

b) Exhorted

(1) Luke 8:14—Jesus said the seed that "fell among thorns are they who, when they have heard [the Word of God], go forth, and are choked with cares and riches and pleasures of this life, and bring no fruit to perfection." People who may look like they have experienced a legitimate conversion show that they were never saved to begin with when they fail to remain in Christ and bear fruit.

(2) 1 John 2:19—"They went out from us, but they were not of us; for if they had been of us, they would no doubt have continued with us; but they went out, that they might be made manifest that they were not all of us." If the church attenders John was talking about had been true believers, they would have stayed involved in Christian fellowship.

(3) 1 John 2:24—"Let that, therefore, abide in you which ye have heard from the beginning. If that which ye have heard from the beginning shall remain in you, ye also shall continue in the Son, and in the Father. And this is the promise that he hath promised us, even eternal life." John says, "You that are for real will remain and inherit eternal life." The abiding believer is the only legitimate believer. When people cease to fellowship with Christians, they give evidence that they never were believers to begin with.

Jesus calls to every apparent disciple to show the reality of his faith by remaining in Him. He makes a black and white distinction: The true believer abides; the nonbeliever—sooner or later—departs.

(4) Colossians 1:21-23—Paul also warned potential Judas-type branches: "And you, that were once alienated and enemies in your mind by wicked works, yet now hath he reconciled in the body of his flesh through death, to present you holy and unblamable and unreprovable in his sight, if ye continue in the faith grounded and settled, and be not moved away from the hope of the gospel, which ye have heard." The Colossians were once sinners apart from God, but Christ died to bring them into a relationship with Him. That relationship needs to be maintained. Paul is saying that the legitimacy of a person's salvation will be determined by his continuance in it.

(5) Hebrews 3:6, 14—"Christ [is] a son over his own house, whose house are we, if we hold fast the confidence and the rejoicing of the hope firm unto the end" (v. 6). The evidence that we are Christ's house will be our continuing faith in Him. Verse 14 says, "For we are made partakers of Christ, if we hold the beginning of our confidence steadfast unto the end." True believers start and end their earthly lives by being vitally connected to Christ (cf. Heb. 10:38-39).

(6) Hebrews 4:14—"Seeing, then, that we have a great high priest, that is passed into the heavens, Jesus, the Son of God, let us hold fast our profession." If you have made a profession of faith in Christ, be sure that you continue to do so. That's the evidence of salvation. When I was in the process of being ordained to serve as a pastor of a church, there was an individual on the ordination council who later became involved in gross immorality and left the ministry. He has totally forsaken any relationship that he ever claimed to have had with Christ. It's obvious that if he were

25

a true believer, he would still be following Christ because that is the character of salvation.

2. The promise (v. 4*b*)

Jesus gives a marvelous promise to the abiding branch: "Abide in me, and I [will remain] in you." Not everyone in the world can claim to experience the constant abiding presence of Jesus Christ—only the one who is constantly abiding in Christ. The New Testament talks about Christians being in Christ and Christ being in them. Colossians 1:27 says, "Christ in you, the hope of glory." We have a relationship with Christ, the Vine. When by real faith we are truly saved, we will always abide and Christ will always abide in us. John 15:4 is a comfort to Christians who might otherwise live in spiritual apoplexy, worrying about hanging onto their salvation. It is also a warning to professing Christians that if they aren't true believers, Christ isn't present in their lives. Many people come to church thinking that just because they show up, the Lord is with them. Being in a church doesn't mean the Lord is with you. He lives in the person of the Spirit within the lives of true disciples. An abiding relationship with Jesus Christ comes only with salvation—genuine faith in Christ. It's a permanent, eternal relationship.

3. The parallels (vv. 8-10)

Jesus repeats the concept of abiding in different ways in verses 8-10.

a) Fruitfulness

In verse 8 Jesus says, "In this is my Father glorified, that ye bear much fruit; so shall ye be my disciples." Jesus is exhorting people to be true disciples, for only they are capable of bearing fruit. He's envisioning fruitless branches that are superficially attached to the Vine. Bearing fruit is equivalent to abiding as a true believer. The unbeliever who is superficially connected to Jesus bears no fruit.

b) Love

In verse 9 Jesus says, "As the Father hath loved me, so have I loved you; continue ye in my love." A true disciple doesn't enter into the love of Christ and then leave it; he continues in it.

c) Obedience

In verse 10 Jesus says, "If ye keep my commandments, ye shall abide in my love, even as I have kept my Father's commandments, and abide in his love." Jesus is again exhorting people to abide in Him.

Abiding, bearing fruit, continuing in Christ's love, and obeying His commandments are different ways of saying the same thing. A true disciple obeys the commandments of Christ and remains in a relationship with Him from the moment of salvation. Since Christ desires true disciples, let's not break His heart as Judas did by failing to abide.

Jesus portrays Himself as the perfect example of abiding. He said, "Even as I have kept my Father's commandments, and abide in His love" (v. 10). Jesus wants the kind of relationship with us that He has with God. In His high priestly prayer in John 17, Christ prays that His disciples might be one with Him and the Father (v. 21). He will never depart from His relationship with the Father, and He wants us to abide with Him in the same way.

In the beginning of John 15, Christ is contrasting the true and the false disciple—the real disciple, who is abiding, and the apparent disciple, who will eventually depart. Christ is pleading with superficial followers to abide, bear fruit, continue in His love, and keep His commandments. Those qualities form a perfect portrait of a true Christian. The true Christian obediently remains in a loving and productive relationship with Jesus Christ; he never leaves. In John 8:31 Jesus says, "If ye continue in my word, then are ye my disciples indeed." A true disciple abides in Christ.

The Simplicity of the Christian Life

In John 14 Jesus says, "If ye love me, [you will] keep my commandments. . . . He that hath my commandments, and keepeth them, he it is that loveth me. . . . If a man love me, he will keep my words" (vv. 15, 21, 23). Every true disciple loves Christ and obeys Him. The two keys to the Christian life are love and obedience. People sometimes think the Christian life is so complicated—do this, do that, sit down, stand up. Christians are simply to love God and others (Matt. 22:37-40), and out of that love will spring obedience to God's Word.

John is contrasting the true and the false disciple. Unbelievers don't abide in Christ, but believers do. All Christians bear fruit, continue in His love, and obey. If someone stops doing those things and forsakes Christ, he never was saved to begin with (1 John 2:19).

B. The Expectation for the Believer

   1. The ideal pattern

      John clearly draws the line between believers and unbelievers throughout his gospel. He doesn't contrast one type of believer from another because he wants to paint an idealistic picture of believers.

      a) Desiring eternal life

         Since believers have eternal life, they will never thirst again for it (John 4:14). But unbelievers will always thirst. Although believers may get a little thirsty in periods of spiritual dryness, John doesn't deal with the exception. Similarly, John 6 records Jesus' promising that the one who believes in Him will never hunger (v. 35). However, as a believer, do you ever get a little bit hungry for spiritual truth? Sure, but John is primarily interested in presenting the ideal pattern designed by God.

      b) Confessing sin

         The book of 1 John illustrates John's style of contrasting various truths (which is a cause of confusion for some). First John 1:8-10 says, "If we say that we have no sin, we deceive ourselves, and the truth is not in us. If we confess our sins, he is faithful and just to forgive us our sins, and cleanse us from all unrighteousness. If we say that we have not sinned, we make him a liar, and his word is not in us." John says believers confess their sins to God, but unbelievers deny their sin. There are occasions when believers don't confess as they should, but John doesn't deal with those. He presents the ideal.

c) Obeying God

First John 2:3-5 says, "By this we do know that we know him, if we keep his commandments. He that saith, I know him, and keepeth not his commandments, is a liar, and the truth is not in him. But whosoever keepeth his word, in him verily is the love of God perfected; by this know we that we are in him." John says unbelievers disobey and believers obey. Do believers ever disobey? Sure, but John doesn't worry about the exceptions.

d) Loving Christians

First John 2:9-11 says, "He that saith he is in the light, and hateth his brother, is in darkness even until now. He that loveth his brother abideth in the light, and there is no occasion of stumbling in him. But he that hateth his brother is in darkness, and walketh in darkness, and knoweth not where he goeth, because darkness hath blinded his eyes." Is there anyone in this world you don't love even though you're a Christian? John says believers always love their brothers, and unbelievers never do. You probably know some believers who don't love their brothers. But remember, John is just trying to make the general lines of distinction clear.

First John 3:14-15 says, "We know that we have passed from death unto life, because we love the brethren. He that loveth not his brother abideth in death. Whosoever hateth his brother is a murderer; and ye know that no murderer hath eternal life abid-

ing in him." It may seem that if a Christian hates someone, he will go to hell, yet John is only drawing the
black and white distinctions.

e) Not loving the world

First John 2:15 says, "Love not the world, neither the
things that are in the world. If any man love the
world, the love of the Father is not in him." There are
probably some things in the world you like very
much. Is John saying you are going to hell because
you want that new car? No.

f) Not sinning

First John 3 says, "Whosoever abideth in him sinneth
not; whosoever sinneth hath not seen him, neither
known him. . . . He that committeth sin is of the devil.
. . . Whosoever is born of God doth not commit sin"
(vv. 6, 8-9).

You may ask, "Didn't John know that some of us Christians might not like some other believer? Didn't he
know we might disobey and sin?" Sure he did, but he
puts the ideals where they belong. He's concerned with
the positional truths and the general patterns of the
Christian life.

2. The realistic perspective

John was aware, however, of the exceptions to the ideal.
First John 2:1 says, "My little children, these things
write I unto you, that ye sin not. And if any man sin, we
have an advocate with the Father, Jesus Christ the righteous." John concedes a little bit so we don't lose sight of
the fact that God knows we'll fail sometimes. There are
general patterns in the Word of God that distinguish a
believer from an unbeliever. John presents them absolutely clear cut. But there are exceptions—times when a
believer sins, hates his brother, disobeys, and fails to
confess his sin.

Therefore, is it reasonable to conclude there are times
when a Christian doesn't abide in the fullest sense? Of

course. But the general pattern of his life will be to abide in Christ. A believer may have a temporary lapse in his relationship with Christ and may cease to abide in the fullest sense. Therefore, the passage in John 15 is not totally restricted to the unbeliever; it could also refer to a believer. Many times in the New Testament we can read commands to love our brothers even though John assumes a believer will always love his brother. Such commands speak to the exceptions to the ideal. For example, Paul's epistles are full of exceptions. The first part of Ephesians talks about a Christian's position—who he is in Christ—and the second part talks about a Christian's practice—what he ought to do. If there weren't any believers who made mistakes, the Father wouldn't have to do any pruning. However, there are exceptions in the lives of Christians when they fail to abide in the fullest sense.

a) The failure

Jesus longs for the believer to abide in Him fully. You may wonder how a Christian could fail to abide. One illustration is found in Galatians 1:6, where Paul writing to Christians says, "I marvel that ye are so soon removed from him that called you into the grace of Christ unto another gospel." When the Galatians started believing legalistic teaching, Paul rebuked them for not abiding. In Galatians 3:3 he says, "Are ye so foolish? Having begun in the Spirit, are ye now made perfect by the flesh?" The Galatians had been saved in the energy of the Holy Spirit, but they were living as if they'd been saved in the energy of the flesh. They believed they needed to keep a list of rules to retain God's acceptance. They had stopped abiding in Christ and started trying to produce their own fruit apart from Him. Legalism is one way a Christian can stop abiding; it is essentially the opposite of abiding.

When Christians fail to abide in the fullest sense of the word, it doesn't mean they lose their salvation. In John 10:27 Jesus says, "My sheep hear my voice, and I know them." You may be a wayward sheep, but you don't turn into a goat (cf. Matt. 25:31-46). When you

31

stop abiding, it doesn't mean you're out of God's love and His kingdom—your position is secure forever. But when you wander a little bit and cease to abide in the fullest sense, you move away from the intimacy of a full relationship with Christ.

To abide as a believer simply means to stay close to Jesus. A branch is much better off if it's connected to the vine. Being only a half inch away from the vine doesn't do a branch any good. To abide is to be totally connected to Jesus Christ in a loving and obedient relationship. As the vine sends its energy through the branch to bear fruit, so Christ can send His energy through you.

b) The feeding

You may say, "I'd like to remain in a close relationship to Jesus. How do I do it?" The beginning of John 15:7 says, "If ye abide in me, and my words abide in you." A believer who is in God's Word is an abiding believer. One who feeds on the truths of the Word of God stays in a close, living, energized relationship with Jesus Christ. Verse 4 says, "As the branch cannot bear fruit of itself, except it abide in the vine, no more can ye, except ye abide in me." A believer should not operate independently of Christ. At some point in their lives, most Christians cease to abide. They independently try to produce their own fruit. Such a person might say, "I'm a very strong and clever branch. I can bear fruit myself. I've produced great fruit before so I know I can do it again." But how much can a detached branch do toward producing fruit? It can't do anything, regardless of its size. The strongest is still helpless and the best is still worthless if it's disconnected from the Vine. Jesus said, "No more can ye [bear fruit], except ye abide in me" (v. 4). Bearing fruit is not a question of whether you're strong or weak, good or bad, brave or cowardly, clever or foolish, experienced or inexperienced. Your gifts, accomplishments, and experience are worthless in helping you produce fruit apart from Jesus Christ. Fruit not produced by Christ is like artificial fruit tied to branches. Even though Paul in Ro-

32

mans 7:18 says, "In my flesh dwelleth no good thing," many Christians have never learned that truth. They run around trying to bear fruit. But you don't bear fruit by trying; you bear it by abiding.

c) The focus

(1) Explained

You abide by recognizing you're a branch and by keeping your position in the Vine. If you want to get as close to Christ as you can, that will involve stripping out the things of the world; putting aside all sin, which distracts and saps your energy; and putting aside the kind of self-effort that operates independently of the Spirit. All those things will rob you of a deep, personal, loving relationship with Jesus. Get into the Word of God, and you'll be an abiding branch. Don't even worry about fruit—just abide, and Christ will produce it through you. Some people say, "I've got to get going; I haven't witnessed in a couple of days!" They just need to get close to Jesus Christ so they can witness in the power of the Spirit. Stay close to Jesus, apart from sin, and in the Word, and you won't ever have to worry about fruit because Christ will produce that as you abide in Him.

(2) Expressed

(a) Galatians 2:20—"I am crucified with Christ: nevertheless I live; yet not I, but Christ liveth in me."

(b) Philippians 2:13—"It is God who worketh in you both to will and to do of his good pleasure." Don't ever worry about the fruit. That's not even your concern. God produces fruit through you as you abide in Christ. The Holy Spirit does not help you bear fruit, and you don't have to help the Holy Spirit bear fruit either. The Holy Spirit can do it all alone. So what are we to do? Nothing. Just abide in Christ.

33

(c) Galatians 3:3—"Having begun in the Spirit, are ye now made perfect by the flesh?" The Galatians started out abiding but soon got misdirected into trusting in their flesh for sanctification.

Have you ever tried to read the Bible and found it boring? When you've witnessed, have you ever felt like you've had ashes in your mouth? Maybe you've prayed in a superficial sense: "Bless the missionaries; now I lay me down to sleep. Amen." You go through the motions but you don't sense any spiritual life. If that's the case, let me encourage you to work on your relationship with Jesus. Don't concentrate on deeds, because they will be the joyful result of that relationship. God wants your life to be fruitful even more than you do. But you can't do one thing yourself to produce it. Just be close to Jesus by being in the Word and by loving and obeying Him, and you will find His energy surging through you to produce fruit. The result will be joy. John 15:11 says, "These things have I spoken unto you, that my joy might remain in you, and that your joy might be full." Would you like to live in the midst of full joy? You say, "What will I have to do? Win eighty-four souls to Christ a month?" No. One thing: abide.

These words in John 15 were spoken by our Lord almost two thousand years ago, but He says them to us today. If you're a superficial Judas-branch, seek to be a true branch—genuinely open your heart and ask Christ in. To the believer He says, "Your general pattern is to abide. Don't let those lapses come. Abide in Me in the fullest sense, and I will produce fruit in you."

Focusing on the Facts

1. What does Jesus use the analogy of a vine and branch to teach His disciples about (see p. 22)?
2. What does Jesus want His superficial followers to do (see p. 23)?
3. What does the word "abide" mean? In the context of John 15, what is abiding in Christ evidence of (see pp. 23-24)?

4. What effect can worldly cares and riches have on someone who has initially responded to God's Word with a measure of faith (Luke 8:14; see p. 24)?
5. If a church attender discontinues his involvement in Christian fellowship, what does he give evidence of? Why (1 John 2:19; see pp. 24)?
6. Is our reconciliation with God mentioned in Colossians 1:23 conditional? Explain (see p. 25).
7. What is the promise Jesus gives to those who abide in Him, according to John 15:4 (see p. 26)?
8. What are three parallel manifestations of abiding (see p. 26-27)?
9. How is Jesus the perfect example of abiding (John 17:21; see p. 27)?
10. What are two keys of the Christian life? Which is a product of the other (John 14:15; see p. 28)?
11. Why doesn't the apostle John emphasize different maturity levels of Christians (see p. 28)?
12. Give some examples of the apostle John's style of contrasting believers and unbelievers (see pp. 28-30).
13. How does the apostle John show his awareness of the exceptions to the ideal pattern for a believer in 1 John 2:1 (see p. 30)?
14. Explain why Jesus' exhortation to abide could apply to believers also (see p. 31).
15. How can a Christian fail to abide (Gal. 1:6; see p. 31-32)?
16. When Christians fail to abide, do they lose their salvation? Explain (John 10:27; see p. 31-32).
17. According to John 15:7, how can we remain in a close relationship with Jesus (see p. 32)?
18. What is the only way a Christian can bear fruit, according to John 15:4 (see p. 32-33)?
19. What types of things can rob us of a deep personal relationship with Jesus (see p. 33)?
20. Does a Christian need to worry about bearing fruit? Explain (see p. 33-34).
21. According to John 15:11, what result can every Christian experience by abiding in Christ (see p. 34)?

Pondering the Principles

1. The apostle John said this about false teachers: "They went out from us, but they were not really of us; for if they had been of us, they would have remained with us; but they went out, in

35

order that it might be shown that they all are not of us" (1 John 2:19, NASB*). Do you know individuals who have disappeared from your congregation? Do you know why they left? If you have wondered what happened to old so-and-so, see if you can track him down and find out how he is doing and why he left. If he was emotionally hurt, encourage him to forgive. If he was attending church for the wrong reasons, explain the purpose for Christian fellowship. If he was confused about spiritual things, give him biblical direction. You may have the opportunity to lead him to Christ, however don't automatically assume he was a unbeliever. He may be a Christian who has had a temporary lapse of abiding in Christ. Your sensitive admonition and instruction may bring him back into fruitful Christian living. Meditate on Romans 15:1-2, 14.

2. Are you abiding in Christ? Or have you slipped into a routine of legalistically grinding out various Christian duties? Evaluate your motivation for your involvement in various Christian activities. Are you in the Word on a regular basis? Do you seek to know more about the One who saved you and whom you claim to follow? Memorize Philippians 3:8-10. Focus on Christ, and you will become a fruitful branch for His glory.

*New American Standard Bible.

3

Abiding in the Vine—Part 2

Outline

Review
I. The Basic Meaning of Abiding (vv. 4, 8-10)

Lesson
II. The Blessings of Abiding (vv. 5, 7-8, 11)
  A. The Fruit of Believers (v. 5)
    1. Its importance
      a) God's plan
        (1) Psalm 1:1-3
        (2) Galatians 5:22-23
      b) God's power
        (1) Hosea 14:8
        (2) Philippians 1:11
    2. Its identity
      a) What it is not
        (1) Success
        (2) Sensationalism
        (3) Simulation
      b) What it is
        (1) Being Christlike
        (2) Praising God
        (3) Contributing to those in need
          (*a*) Philippians 4:17
          (*b*) Romans 15:26, 28
        (4) Communicating spiritual truth
        (5) Doing good works
        (6) Leading others to Christ
          (*a*) John 4:32-36
          (*b*) 1 Corinthians 16:15
          (*c*) Romans 1:13

B. The Faithfulness of God (v. 7)
1. Believing and following Christ (v. 7*a*)
2. Knowing and obeying God's Word (v. 7*b*)
C. The Glory of the Father (v. 8)
1. Stated
2. Supported
   a) Romans 15:18
   b) 1 Peter 2:12
D. The Fullness of Joy (v. 11)
III. The Burning of the Non-Abiding Branches (v. 6)
A. The Casting Forth (v. 6*a*)
B. The Consuming Fire (v. 6*b*)
1. Matthew 13:30, 40-42, 49-50
2. 2 Thessalonians 1:7-9

Review

Jesus is in the upper room in John 15. He speaks about two types of disciples: the eleven before Him, who are real disciples, and Judas, who has gone to betray Him. In this context, He draws an allegory of the vine and the branches. He is the Vine, the Father is the Vinedresser, and the branches are followers of Jesus—some of them are real and some are not. He tells us that you can discern which followers are true believers because they will bear fruit, obey, continue in His love, and remain in a close relationship with Him. False believers do none of those things and only follow Jesus temporarily. That is why Christ warns superficial followers of the terrible tragedy of being around Him like Judas but not being saved.

The imperative to abide is an exhortation to unbelievers, yet it also applies to Christians. In a positional sense, we do abide in Christ—that is the character of being saved. But there's a sense in which Christians fail to abide as fully as they ought to. We're always in fellowship with the Father and the Son, because fellowship means partnership, and nothing can ever break that if we're saved. However, we lose the joy and the experience of that fellowship when we temporarily cease to abide in a close relationship with Christ.

A man has two choices: He can be a Christian, one who truly abides in Christ; or he can be an unbeliever, one who fails to bear fruit, continue in Christ's love, obey His commands, and therefore ends in ultimate and eternal disaster. I want to examine the consequences of being a true branch connected to Christ and the consequences of being one that is cast aside. If you are struggling between giving your life to Jesus Christ or keeping your distance from Him and just being religious, I hope you will choose Christ.

I. THE BASIC MEANING OF ABIDING (vv. 4, 8-10; see pp. 23-34)

Lesson

II. THE BLESSINGS OF ABIDING (vv. 5, 7-8, 11)

A true disciple, one who really commits his life to Jesus Christ, is blessed. The one who has a loving relationship with Christ and in whom Christ's dwells is the one through whom Christ bears fruit.

A. The Fruit of Believers (v. 5)

"I am the vine, ye are the branches. He that abideth in me, and I in him, the same bringeth forth much fruit; for without me ye can do nothing."

There can't be any fruit on a branch that doesn't remain on the Vine. Only an abiding branch will bring forth good fruit. So every Christian bears fruit; there is no such thing as a fruitless Christian. Jesus said, "Every good tree bringeth forth good fruit" (Matt. 7:17). Jesus even said you can tell whether a man is saved or not by his fruit: "Ye shall know them by their fruits" (Matt. 7:16). He says basically the same thing in John 15:5. Although it may be difficult to find, there will always be fruit in the life of a believer. There may be lapses when he doesn't experience the fullness of abiding in Christ, but there will be fruit in his life because the indwelling Christ will produce it.

1. Its importance

Fruit is important. You may say, "Why bother with it? If I'm saved, why shouldn't I just hang around until I go to

39

heaven?" Because God wants you to have a productive life, He produces fruit through your life by His own power. Two facts indicate its importance:

a) God's plan

    (1) Psalm 1:1-3—"Blessed is the man who walketh not in the counsel of the ungodly, nor standeth in the way of sinners, nor sitteth in the seat of the scornful. But his delight is in the law of the Lord; and in his law doth he meditate day and night. And he shall be like a tree planted by the rivers of water, that bringeth forth its fruit in its season." Even in the Old Testament, the godly man was considered a fruit-bearing man. God was in him producing fruit.

    (2) Galatians 5:22-23—The apostle Paul said, "The fruit of the Spirit is love, joy, peace, long-suffering, gentleness, goodness, faith, meekness, self-control." Fruit is an expected result in the life of a godly man or woman by God's design. It is the product of God's life within believers, whether in the Old Testament or the New.

b) God's power

Fruit is also important because God is its enabling source. A man is not the source of fruit; he's merely the branch. It is God who produces life; it is His power that produces fruit.

    (1) Hosea 14:8—In the Old Testament God says, "From me is thy fruit found." Fruit is from God, and only the person or the branch that abides in God has the divine resource to bear good fruit.

    (2) Philippians 1:11—Paul talked about fruit from the standpoint of salvation, saying we are to be "filled with the fruits of righteousness, which are by Jesus Christ." There can't be any righteousness unless a man is born again and receives the righteousness of Christ. The only way you'll ever have fruit is to be saved because the fruit in you is

the product of Christ in you. In John 10:37-38, Jesus says that the Father is working through Him.

2. Its identity

a) What it is not

(1) Success

Nowhere in the Bible is success ever synonymous with fruit. Some people think that if something is big and there are many people involved in it, it must be blessed by God. However, that is no guarantee that it is divinely produced fruit. For example, the ministry of a missionary shouldn't be evaluated solely on the basis of whether it looks like he has been successful. His many years of ministry may have been valuable years of planting and watering (1 Cor. 3:5-8), although they may not show much harvesting. At the same time, successful-looking missionary work may have been the result of fleshly performance with little good fruit. You cannot effectively measure fruit by success.

(2) Sensationalism

Not only should you avoid measuring the fruitfulness of a ministry by the number of people who have been won to the Lord or who attend a church, but you should also avoid measuring it by the evidence of emotionalism or zealousness for some program. That's not fruit either.

(3) Simulation

True fruit produced by God through us cannot be simulated. There's a subtle danger of some believers trying to do externally what the Spirit of God has produced internally through the lives of other believers. We all aren't the same kind of branch in the sense that we produce the same kind of fruit. Every believer bears fruit that is in a sense unique, though it's common to all of us. It's easy for someone to set out on a course of self-improvement, in which he's trying to be like someone else rather than abiding in Christ and letting God produce the fruit. If a Christian starts simulating someone else's fruit, he has violated the basic principle of abiding because he has produced artificial fruit. Fruit comes by abiding in Christ.

b) What it is

(1) Being Christlike

A believer who is like Christ bears fruit. His life is patterned after Christ. That is the implication of Galatians 5:22-23, where Paul says, "The fruit of the Spirit is love, joy, peace, long-suffering, gentleness, goodness, faith, meekness, self-control; against such there is no law." All those virtues, without exception, were characteristics of Jesus Christ. As Christians, we are to reproduce the life of Christ in us as we abide in Him. Jesus was known by His love, His peace, and His joy, all of which He gave to His disciples (John 14:21, 27; 15:11). Everything He has He gives to those who are His.

You may wonder if there is any spiritual fruit in your life. If there's any love, joy, or peace in your life, the answer is yes. The fruit of the Spirit becomes part of your life only as you abide in Christ. You don't need to work on each of them one at a time. By the time you get to the end of the list, you've probably lost your love, peace, and joy that you worked on first, so you've got to start all over again. What you really need to do is abide in Christ. Be concerned about the quality of your relationship to Jesus and the fruit will come by itself.

(2) Praising God

Offering praise to Christ is fruit. Hebrews 13:15 says, "By him, therefore, let us offer the sacrifice

42

of praise to God continually, that is, the fruit of our lips giving thanks to his name." A worshipful, thankful spirit is one kind of fruit. When you express adoration to Christ and thank Him for all that He has given you, you are offering Him fruit.

(3) Contributing to those in need

We usually don't think about supplying a need for someone as being fruit, but it is.

(a) Philippians 4:17—The apostle Paul had received a gift from the church at Philippi while he was imprisoned in Rome. He thanked them, saying, "Not because I desire a gift; but I desire fruit that may abound to your account." He's saying, "It's not that I want a present; it's that I love to see the fruit of your relationship to Christ."

(b) Romans 15:26, 28—Paul considered the financial support given by converted Gentiles to Jewish believers to be fruit of their loving generosity: "It hath pleased them of Macedonia and Achaia to make a certain contribution for the poor saints who are at Jerusalem. . . . When, therefore, I have performed this, and have sealed to them this fruit, I will come by you into Spain." Their monetary gift was representative of their love. A contribution out of love to those in need is a form of spiritual fruit.

(4) Communicating spiritual truth

Sharing spiritual truths with others is another type of fruit. First Corinthians 14:14 addresses the issue of speaking in tongues while praying: "If I pray in an unknown tongue, my spirit prayeth, but my understanding is unfruitful." If a Christian prays in a language that no one knows, he is unable to comprehend its meaning and cannot contribute anything to the rest of the church by it. There is no fruit in that. The Christian who is in tune with the Spirit will think of others first and will pray with his understanding that he might impart to them spiritual truth. Communication that blesses others is fruit. This principle may apply in other areas as well. For example, a believer can study the Bible by himself and never bother to share it with anyone else. That's fruitless in the sense that what he has learned is not being communicated to bless other people.

(5) Doing good works

In Colossians 1:10, Paul prays that the Colossians might be fruitful: "Walk worthy of the Lord unto all pleasing, being fruitful in every good work." Good works are fruit.

(6) Leading others to Christ

People won to Jesus Christ through witnessing are also the fruit of abiding. As you abide in Christ, opportunities will arise and fruit will result. Concentrate on your relationship to Jesus Christ, and He'll determine which fruit is ready to be picked. Don't get yourself tied in knots because you haven't led a certain amount of people to the Lord. The way to win people to Jesus Christ is not to be legalistic about it but to abide in Him.

(a) John 4:32-36—On His way to Galilee, Jesus passed through Samaria and met a woman at a well in the village of Sychar. While she went into town to tell the people of her meeting with Jesus, His disciples encouraged Him to eat. "But he said unto them, I have food to eat that ye know not of. Therefore said the disciples one to another, Hath any man brought him anything to eat? Jesus saith unto them, My food is to do the will of him that sent me, and to finish his work. Say not ye, There are yet four months, and then cometh harvest? Behold, I say unto you, Lift up your eyes, and look on the fields; for they are

44

white already to harvest" (vv. 32-35). As Jesus spoke these words, He could see the white-robed people from the village of Sychar visible above the tops of the grain in the fields. Continuing His analogy, in verse 36 He says, "He that reapeth receiveth wages, and gathereth fruit unto life eternal." So Jesus identified converts as a kind of fruit.

(b) 1 Corinthians 16:15—Paul identified the family of Stephanas as the first converts in Achaia: "I beseech you, brethren (ye know the house of Stephanas, that it is the first fruits of Achaia, and that they have devoted themselves to the ministry of the saints)."

(c) Romans 1:13—It's possible that Paul was referring to converts when he told the Roman Christians, "I purposed to come unto you . . . that I might have some fruit among you."

So Christ enables Christians to bear fruit as they remain intimately involved with Him. It's a marvelous thing to realize all the kinds of fruit that Christ produces in us as we abide. If we're not enjoying fruit in our lives, then we aren't abiding as God designed us to.

B. The Faithfulness of God (v. 7)

"If ye abide in me, and my words abide in you, ye shall ask what ye will, and it shall be done unto you."

The faithfulness of God in answering prayer is another blessing of abiding in Christ. God says, "If you are truly an abiding branch, I will be faithful to answer every prayer." That's a fantastic promise! I want you to realize, however, that there are two conditions that allow God to respond.

1. Believing and following Christ (v. 7a)

"If ye abide in me."

The first condition for answered prayer is being a true believer. The word translated "abide" (Gk., *meinete*) is used here in the aorist tense and implies in this context a permanent fact. You must be a permanently abiding branch—a true believer. The mark of a true Christian is that he abides. Such a person will experience the blessing of having his prayers answered. God is under no obligation, however, to answer the prayers of unbelievers. You ask, "Does God ever answer their prayers?" Yes, He does. He may do that in His own sovereign design, but He makes no promises that He will do so, especially in the case of a false believer like Judas.

2. Knowing and obeying God's Word (v. 7b)

"And my words abide in you."

The second condition for answered prayer is letting the Word of God abide in you. If Jesus had commanded you to abide in Him without adding the condition of letting His Word direct your prayers, that would be a blank check signed by God to pray for anything and get it. If you've asked God for many things that He didn't give you, you might check on whether His words are abiding in you. If your life is continually regulated by the God's Word, the Lord will answer your prayers. The "words" (Gk., *rēmata*) that Jesus was referring to were His specific utterances, rather than his making broader reference to the Bible. The individual words of Christ have to be controlling our lives. It's easy to say we pattern our lives after the Word of God in a general way. However, it is much more difficult to pattern out lives after the practical teaching of Jesus. That involves studying the truths of the Word and obeying God's will. Learning and applying the truths Christ has revealed through the writers of the New Testament makes it possible for God to respond to our prayers because we are being controlled by Christ's words.

Jesus indicates the same principle in John 14:13-14: "Whatever ye shall ask in my name, that will I do. . . . If ye shall ask anything in my name, I will do it." When you pray for something in the name of Jesus, it means you pray with Him in mind; it doesn't mean you merely attach the words *in Jesus' name* at the end of your prayers. It means you are praying consistently with the words and the will of Jesus Christ. From another angle, when you get a positive answer to your prayer, you can be sure you have asked according to His Word and will. The Christian who abides in Christ and is being controlled by the Lord's words will not ask anything contrary to the Lord's will because His Word and His will are always consistent.

Your prayers should reflect this spirit: "I'm asking this, Father, because I know it is the will of Jesus Christ. I'm asking this for His sake, knowing He would like it to be done." When you can say that, then you're asking according to His will. Unfortunately, it's very easy to ask for something that's not according to His will. James 4:3 says, "Ye ask, and receive not, because ye ask amiss, that ye may consume it upon your lusts." It's one thing to say I want what Jesus wants because my life is controlled by His precepts; it's something completely different to say I want what I desire in spite of what God thinks—that's being overly independent and selfish. But if you meet the two conditions of following Christ and obeying His Word, God will answer every prayer you bring before Him. His faithfulness is a promise.

C. The Glory of the Father (v. 8)

"In this is my Father glorified, that ye bear much fruit."

1. Stated

A believer who abides in Christ and bears fruit brings honor to God. Christians are here on this earth to do one thing: to give God the glory that He deserves. Everything that is produced in our lives by the Spirit is fruit that gives glory to the Father—not to us.

2. Supported

   a) Romans 15:18—"I will not dare to speak of any of those things which Christ hath not wrought by me." Paul didn't go around telling people how good he was; he was only interested in telling about the things that Christ did through him. In Galatians 2:20 Paul says, "I am crucified with Christ: nevertheless I live; yet not I, but Christ liveth in me." As we yield to Him, He fulfills His will through us.

b) 1 Peter 2:12—"[Have] your behavior honest among the Gentiles, that, whereas they speak against you as evildoers, they may by your good works, which they shall behold, glorify God." Whatever is produced in your life by His Spirit gives Him glory. Wouldn't you like to glorify the Father? As you abide in Christ, He can produce more fruit in you so the Father can be further glorified.

D. The Fullness of Joy (v. 11)

"These things have I spoken unto you, that my joy might remain in you, and that your joy might be full."

John 15:1-10, which deals with abiding in Christ, bearing fruit, answered prayer, and continuing in Christ's love and obeying Him as true disciples, points to one final climactic blessing: full joy. What a tremendous promise! Unfortunately, some think living the Christian life is monastic deprivation, some kind of a bitter religious pill that they have to swallow. Actually, every bit of the Christian life is designed for our joy. However, the Christian who violates the things mentioned in John 15 isn't joyous. If you want full joy, then you must abide in Christ in the fullest sense.

Jesus wanted the joy He experienced in fellowship with the Father to remain in His disciples. In verse 10 He says, "If ye keep my commandments, ye shall abide in my love, even as I have kept my Father's commandments, and abide in his love." Jesus is the example of the perfect abiding life resulting in full joy. In the midst of all that Jesus suffered, He still had full joy because of His abiding relationship with the Father. When you abide in Him, you'll have the same joy.

When David sinned and no longer sensed the presence of God, he cried out, "Restore unto me the joy of thy salvation" (Ps. 51:12). He didn't lose his salvation; he just lost the joy of it because he had ceased to abide in the fullest sense.

Peter refers to abiding joy as "joy unspeakable and full of

48

glory" (1 Pet. 1:8). That's the kind of joy that Jesus had, and that's the kind of joy that can belong to any Christian. A Christian's joy should be so full that it has a controlling influence on the rest of his life. Unfortunately, I don't know too many Christians like that. I meet many grouchy Christians who don't experience joy because they aren't fully abiding in Christ. A Christian who is temporarily not abiding is usually easy to identify by his negative, defeated attitude.

When you hear the blessings of abiding in Christ, I don't know how anyone could say no to Jesus Christ. Sadly, for those who do, there is an alternative to those blessings.

III. THE BURNING OF THE NON-ABIDING BRANCHES (v. 6)

A. The Casting Forth (v. 6a)

"If a man abide not in me, he is cast forth as a branch, and is withered."

The non-believing follower of Christ will be cast forth. He has no living connection with Jesus Christ. If he were a true believer, that wouldn't happen. In John 6:37 Jesus says, "Him that cometh to me I will in no wise cast out." The true disciple is never cast out, but the one who was never was real to begin with is. Notice that apart from Christ, the false disciple withers. Whatever faint glimpses of life he acquired by being superficially attached to Christ disappear when he is separated from the Vine. He's like the seed that fell on stony ground and sprang up for a little while but then dried up (Matt. 13:5-6, 20-21).

B. The Consuming Fire (v. 6b)

"Men gather them, and cast them into the fire, and they are burned."

That is a picture of judgment. God's instruments of judgment are none other than His holy angels.

1. Matthew 13:30, 40-42, 49-50—Jesus said, "Let [the wheat and the tares] grow together until the harvest; and in the time of harvest I will say to the reapers, Gath-

er together first the tares, and bind them in bundles to burn them, but gather the wheat into my barn" (v. 30). We see that the "reapers" on Judgment Day are angels from verses 40-42 and 49-50: "As, therefore, the tares are gathered and burned in the fire, so shall it be in the end of this age. The Son of man shall send forth his angels, and they shall gather out of his kingdom all things that offend, and them who do iniquity, and shall cast them into a furnace of fire; there shall be wailing and gnashing of teeth. . . . So shall it be at the end of the age; the angels shall come forth, and separate the wicked from among the righteous, and shall cast them into the furnace of fire; there shall be wailing and gnashing of teeth." Christ will send His angels to cast the ungodly and unrighteous into hell for eternity. Judas-like branches will burn there forever. That's the choice that every man has to make.

2. 2 Thessalonians 1:7-9—"To you who are troubled, rest with us, when the Lord Jesus shall be revealed from heaven with his mighty angels, in flaming fire taking vengeance on them that know not God, and obey not the gospel of our Lord Jesus Christ; who shall be punished with everlasting destruction from the presence of the Lord, and from the glory of his power." There is coming a day when God is going to send His angels to gather the ungodly from around the world and cast them into an eternal hell. How tragic to appear like a believer but to end up in hell separated from Christ for eternity!

Peter gave this warning about people who have superficially attached themselves to Jesus: "If, after they have escaped the pollutions of the world through the knowledge of the Lord and Savior, Jesus Christ, they are again entangled in [the world], and overcome, the latter end is worse with them than the beginning. For it had been better for them not to have known the way of righteousness than, after they have known it, to turn from the holy commandment delivered unto them. But it is happened unto them according to the true proverb, The dog is turned to his own vomit again; and the sow that was washed, to her wallowing in the mire" (2 Pet. 2:20-22). The worst thing that could ever happen would be to know about Jesus but never commit your life to Him. Eternal retribution for such a person will be more severe than for the person who didn't know

Him at all. Every man has a choice: He can abide in the Vine and receive blessing, or he can be separated from the Vine and burned.

Focusing on the Facts

1. When do Christians lose the joy of their relationship with Christ (see p. 38-39)?
2. Will every Christian bear fruit? Support your answer with Scripture (see p. 39).
3. Why is being fruitful important (see pp. 39-40)?
4. Is fruitfulness necessarily associated with success? Give an example (see p. 41).
5. As Christians, we are to reproduce the life of _____ in us as we _____ in Him (see p. 42).
6. Be concerned with the _____ of your relationship to Christ and the _____ will come by itself (see p. 42).
7. What kind of fruit does Hebrews 13:15 say we should continually offer to God (see pp. 42-43)?
8. What kind of fruit had Paul collected from the Gentiles to take back to Jewish believers (Rom. 15:26, 28; see pp. 43)?
9. To be an effective soul winner, what should a Christian concentrate on (see pp. 44-45)?
10. What two conditions allow God to respond to our prayers (see pp. 45-47)?
11. Does God ever answer the prayers of unbelievers? Explain (see p. 46).
12. Explain what it means to pray in the name of Jesus (see pp. 46-47).
13. Why will a Christian who abides in Christ and is controlled by the Lord's words not pray for anything contrary to His will (see p. 47)?
14. What is the reason that some Christians' prayers are not answered, according to James 4:3 (see p. 47)?
15. What is the primary thing Christians are on this earth to do (see p. 47)?
16. According to 1 Peter 2:12, what can help transform unbelievers from slanderers to those who glorify God (see p. 48)?
17. What type of joy did Jesus want His disciples to experience (John 15:11; see p. 48)?
18. When David temporarily ceased abiding and therefore sinned, what did he lose (Ps. 51:12; see p. 48)?

19. According to John 15:6, what happens to the person who is superficially attached to Christ? Why can't that happen to a Christian? Support your answer with Scripture (see p. 49).
20. In the words of 2 Thessalonians 1:7-9, describe the ultimate destiny of those who "obey not the gospel of the Lord Jesus Christ" (v. 8; see p. 50).
21. For whom will eternal retribution be more severe (see p. 50-51)?

Pondering the Principles

1. Review the various kinds of fruit mentioned on pages 42-45. Which kinds of fruit do you find presently in your life? Which are missing or need to be nourished? How would you evaluate the manner in which you are abiding in Christ? Are you communing with the Lord regularly though prayer and Bible reading? As you focus on improving your relationship with Christ, look for opportunities to apply the fruit He produces to those situations. Memorize Colossians 1:10: "Walk in a manner worthy of the Lord, to please Him in all respects, bearing fruit in every good work and increasing in the knowledge of God" (NASB).

2. Do you know grumpy Christians? Do you know Christians who cover themselves with a protective facade by trying to be positive all the time? Those kinds of Christians are not prepared for the trials that are guaranteed to confront us in life. They lack the greatest personal blessing of abiding in Christ: full joy. Few Christians probably experience the joy that the apostle Paul did. He understood the importance, privilege, and benefits of abiding in Christ (Phil. 3:7-14). That is why he could say in the midst of his imprisonment, "Rejoice in the Lord always; again I will say, rejoice! . . . Be anxious for nothing. . . . I have learned to be content in whatever circumstances I am. . . . I can do all things through Him who strengthens me. . . . My God shall supply all your needs according to His riches" (Phil. 4:4, 6, 11, 13, 19, NASB). His joy was a product of His abiding in a God who sovereignly "causes all things to work together for good" (Rom. 8:28, NASB) and who "will not allow you to be tempted beyond what you are able [to endure]" (1 Cor. 10:13, NASB). Meditate on Hebrews 12:1-4. Are your eyes fixed on Jesus?

4

The Friends of Jesus

Outline

Introduction
A. The Comfort of Friendship with Jesus
B. The Characteristics of Friendship with Jesus
C. The Condition of Friendship with Jesus
   1. John 15:10
   2. 1 John 3:9-10
   3. John 10:27
   4. John 8:31

Lesson
I. Friends of Jesus Love Each Other (vv. 12-14)
   A. The Command About Love (vv. 12, 14)
      1. Stated
      2. Supported
         a) Romans 5:5
         b) 1 John 2:9-11
         c) 1 John 5:1
         d) 1 Thessalonians 4:9
   B. The Comparison Regarding Love (v. 13)
      1. Explained
      2. Exercised
      3. Exemplified
      4. Exhorted
II. Friends of Jesus Know Divine Truth (v. 15)
   A. Stated
   B. Supported
      1. John 8:31-32
      2. John 17:6-8
      3. Matthew 13:10-11
      4. Luke 10:23-24

53

Introduction

The friendship that Christians have with Jesus is absolutely amazing, especially when we realize that we can have a personal, intimate relationship with the Son of God, who is responsible for creating and upholding the universe. It's overwhelming to grasp what it means to be a friend of Jesus Christ.

James made the statement that "friendship with the world is hostility toward God" (4:4, NASB). A man chooses during his life whether he will be the friend of Jesus Christ or the friend of the world. Being a friend of Christ involves fellowship with the Trinity and "inexpressible and glorious joy" (1 Pet. 1:8, NIV*).

*New International Version.

A. The Comfort of Friendship with Jesus

In John 15, Jesus talks to His eleven beloved disciples after Judas left to betray Him (John 13:21-30). The eleven are represented by the abiding branches in the analogy Jesus describes in the preceding verses of chapter 15. Aware of the impending departure of Jesus, their hearts were filled with sorrow. But Jesus comforted them by telling them they were His personal, intimate, and beloved friends.

B. The Characteristics of Friendship with Jesus

In John 15:15 Jesus says, "Henceforth I call you not servants; for the servant knoweth not what his lord doeth: but I have called you friends." Friendship is the theme of the next several verses. Jesus identifies His true disciples—the abiding, fruit-bearing believers—as friends in the fullest sense of all that the word implies. That sense of intimacy is conveyed by several other terms. In the New Testament, believers are called "sons of God" (Rom. 8:19) and "children of God" (1 John 3:1). We are considered as important as the brothers, sisters, and mother of Jesus (Mark 3:35) and are called His brethren (Heb. 2:11). Believers are also called "disciples" (Gk., *mathētēs*, "learners"; John 8:31) and "sheep" (John 10:27). All those terms picture varying degrees of intimacy that a believer has with Christ. The dimensions of that loving relationship will be limited by your understanding of Jesus Christ Himself.

The special meaning implied in being "friends" in verse 15 is seen in comparison to being "servants" (Gk., *douloi*, "slaves"). No longer considering them servants, Jesus elevated them to the position of friends. A servant was not a position of shame; the term *servant* was often used to refer to people who served God. For example, Moses, Joshua, and David were referred to as servants of God. In the New Testament, both Paul and James counted it an honor to be "a servant of God" (Titus 1:1; James 1:1). But Jesus said, "I have something greater for you yet: an intimate relationship with Me as friends." In the Old Testament, only Abraham was called the "friend" of God (Isa. 41:8). He had a unique relationship to God as the father of Israel. But Jesus bestows a unique intimacy on New Testament believers—friendship.

C. The Condition of Friendship with Jesus

In John 15:14, Jesus gives a clear-cut condition for being His friend: "Ye are my friends, if ye do whatever I command you." The key to being a friend of Jesus is obedience. In fact, obedience is the standard for every relationship with Him.

1. John 15:10—"If ye keep my commandments, ye shall abide in my love." The abiding believer is obedient.

2. 1 John 3:9-10—"Whosoever is born of God doth not commit sin; for his seed remaineth in him, and he cannot sin, because he is born of God. In this the children of God are manifest, and the children of the devil: whosoever doeth not righteousness is not of God, neither he that loveth not his brother." Obeying God's righteous standards and loving our brothers are two of the commands of Jesus. You do not, however, become a child of God by obedience; your obedience gives evidence that you are God's child. Obedience is the proof that you are intimately connected to Jesus Christ.

3. John 10:27—Jesus said of the believers who followed Him, "My sheep hear my voice, and I know them, and they follow me." Obedience is the standard of a relationship to Jesus Christ.

4. John 8:31—"Then said Jesus to those Jews who believed on him, If ye continue in my word, then are ye my disciples indeed." In every case where the New Testament talks about a relationship to Jesus Christ, that relationship is made visible by obedience. A true disciple will obey Christ. Obedience is also the mark of a friend of Jesus. The world can tell who we are because we obey Him.

Be a Name-Dropper

Friendship with Jesus is a fantastic privilege. Next time you're in a group where someone is dropping the names of

Lesson

In John 15:12-16, Jesus gives five characteristics of His friends.
They are not things you must do to become a friend of Jesus;
they are the visible evidence that you are already His friend.
The friends of Jesus love each other, know divine truth, are
chosen out of this world, bear fruit that remains, and have
their prayers answered. The idea of all those things belonging
to the believer is almost beyond imagination.

I. FRIENDS OF JESUS LOVE EACH OTHER (vv. 12-13)

A. The Command About Love (vv. 12, 14)

"This is my commandment, that ye love one another, as I
have loved you. . . . Ye are my friends, if ye do whatever I
command you."

1. Stated

The obedient believer is a friend of Jesus who has a sin-
cere love for other believers. Granted there are some exceptions, but John is not concerned about them. Jesus
commands us to keep on loving each other. A Christian's
love for others is the greatest thing to have in a world
that is starving for love. Our hearts should be full of
love.

2. Supported

a) Romans 5:5—"The love of God is shed abroad in our
hearts." Christians experience the love of God. What
a tremendous privilege! The true believer will share
that love with others. You can't be a true believer in
Christ and not have a love for others.

b) 1 John 2:9-11—"He that saith he is in the light, and
hateth his brother, is in darkness even until now. He

57

that loveth his brother abideth in the light, and there is no occasion of stumbling in him. But he that hateth his brother is in darkness, and walketh in darkness, and knoweth not where he goeth, because darkness hath blinded his eyes." The true believer doesn't hate his brother.

c) 1 John 5:1—"Whosoever believeth that Jesus is the Christ is born of God; and everyone that loveth him that begot loveth him also that is begotten of him." A man is saved and becomes a friend of Jesus when he believes that Jesus is the Christ. His love for the Father will also be expressed in his love for Christ and others who have been born again spiritually. There's no such thing as loving God without loving Christ and other believers. It is characteristic of a true friend of Jesus that he loves the other friends of Jesus.

d) 1 Thessalonians 4:9—"As touching brotherly love, ye need not that I write unto you; for ye yourselves are taught of God to love one another." Part of being a believer is loving other believers. In fact, a friend of Jesus would violate his nature in Christ if he didn't love others. It's natural for a believer to love the other friends of Jesus; only sin prevents such love.

The world doesn't know much about the quality of love that Christians experience because "the love of Christ . . . surpasses knowledge" (Eph. 3:19, NASB). Although the friends of Jesus fellowship in His love, there are occasionally some flaws in how they express it. Nevertheless, the general pattern of Christians is that they love one other. As we abide in Christ, we experience the fruit of the Spirit, part of which is love. If you don't love others, the problem is not resolved by conjuring up love yourself. It is resolved only by getting close to Jesus so that love becomes a fruit produced by Him through you, the abiding branch.

B. The Comparison Regarding Love (v. 13)

"Greater love hath no man than this, that a man lay down his life for his friends."

1. Explained

Jesus says in verse 12, "Love one another, as I have loved you." Now, you can't love to the point of redeeming the whole world, but you can love with a sacrificial kind of love that gives. God isn't expecting you to love with a dimension of love equal to Christ's. He is expecting your love to have a sacrificial nature as Christ's did. His disciples are not merely to be devoted and helpful to each other. We are to love as Jesus loved, giving of ourselves. Don't look at your brother in Christ as someone who's only an acquaintance; rather see him as Jesus would—primarily in terms of his soul's eternal needs. That requires the kind of love that is involved in comforting, instructing, and bearing one another's burdens. Sometimes we substitute a superficial relationship for one that is deep. We need to intimately care about the needs of others.

2. Exercised

Sacrificial love is important to our testimony. Jesus told His disciples, "By this shall all men know that ye are my disciples, if ye have love one to another" (John 13:35). We show the world who we are by reaching into the heart and soul of someone and giving of our time, wealth, encouragement, and empathy—whatever the needs may be. The fullest kind of love is described in verse 13: "Greater love hath no man than this, that a man lay down his life for his friends." Our love for others is to be so intense, that if need be, it would lead us to die for someone else. The world over has acknowledged that as the supreme evidence of love.

3. Exemplified

In the case of Jesus, He loved so sacrificially that He laid down His life. If He hadn't died, everyone who has ever lived would spend forever in hell because there would be no sacrifice for sin. He knew He was not dying for Himself but for mankind by bearing our sins in His own body on the cross. Second Corinthians 5:21 says that

God has made Christ, "who knew no sin, to be sin for us, that we might be made the righteousness of God in him." Christ died a substitutionary death, and we are the beneficiaries. We're not just witnesses of Calvary. We're the recipients of what was accomplished there; we reap the benefit of His life and willing surrender in death.

It's difficult to imagine the kind of love that would die for another, but even the world knows of it to some extent. Charles Dickens, in the classic story *A Tale of Two Cities*, tells us about the character Charles Darnay, who was caught up in the swirl of the French Revolution. Although personally blameless, he was unjustly found guilty. While in prison to await the guillotine, a friend resembling him by the name Sydney Carton secretly drugged him, exchanged clothes, and took his place at the guillotine the next morning, while friends removed the drugged body of Darnay. His life was spared because his friend died for him.

That kind of love—the willingness to totally sacrifice oneself—should be common among believers. Certainly it has been seen among missionaries who have died to take the gospel to others. However, some of us don't even love others enough to give our time to someone, let alone our lives. Sometimes we neglect to share our love with our neighbors who need to know the truth of Jesus Christ, or minister our gifts to other believers who aren't growing, or give to needs around the world where money is needed for ministries to be carried on. Some of us haven't even learned to live for others, let alone die for them. Yet Jesus died for us when we hated Him. Paul said, "Perhaps for a good man some would even dare to die. But God commendeth his love toward us in that, while we were yet sinners, Christ died for us" (Rom. 5:7-8). That is the greatest example of sacrificial love for unlovable people. When we begin to love like that, the world is going to be in a state of shock and will listen to our message.

4. Exhorted

Have you ever given of yourself in a spirit of sacrifice to meet someone else's need? First John 3:16-18 forces us to examine the depth of our love: "By this perceive we the love of God, because he laid down his life for us" (v. 16). We know God loves us because He laid down the life of His Son for our benefit. If you could ask God how much He loves you, I believe He'd point to a rocky hillside outside Jerusalem and say, "On that hill two thousand years ago My beloved Son died. That's how much I love you." At the end of verse 16, John exhorts us to demonstrate that same kind of love: "We ought to lay down our lives for the brethren." Are you ready to do that? Do you really care about others that deeply? Have you looked around to see who has spiritual and physical needs and then ministered to them in love? If not, then verses 17-18 are for you: "But whosoever hath this world's good, and seeth his brother have need, and shutteth up his compassions from him, how dwelleth the love of God in him? My little children, let us not love in word, neither in tongue, but in deed and in truth." If you see a fellow believer with a need you can meet, but don't, you are failing to express God's love. We talk about His love so freely, but we are often afraid of going a step further and giving it away. We need to be reminded that the friends of Jesus love each other sacrificially, as He loved them.

II. FRIENDS OF JESUS KNOW DIVINE TRUTH (v. 15)

A. Stated

The friends of Jesus know divine truth. When I stop to realize that, I am amazed because I am aware of my own intellectual limitations. A Christian can actually know the truths of the universe! Verse 15 says, "Henceforth I call you not servants; for the servant knoweth not what his lord doeth: but I have called you friends, for all things that I have heard of my Father I have made known unto you." The slave could never be a friend because the ancient Greco-Roman culture had reduced the slave to a living tool. His master never told him his goals and desires; he just told him what to do. Slaves serve because they are required to do so to earn their keep. They rarely are concerned about their master's wishes, but serve out of duty and fear.

But we who are Jesus' friends are not blindly obeying; we share His heart and purposes. Our greatest desire is to ac-

61

complish God's will. We're not working to earn anything; we're working because it's our heart's desire to be a part of His plan, which He's revealed to us—past, present, and future.

B. Supported

1. John 8:31-32—"Then said Jesus to those Jews who believed on him, If ye continue in my word, then are ye my disciples indeed; and ye shall know the truth." Christians have a knowledge of divine truth.

2. John 17:6-8—Jesus said to the Father, "I have manifested thy name unto the men whom thou gavest me out of the world; thine they were, and thou gavest them to me, and they have kept thy word. Now they have known that all things, whatever thou hast given me, are of thee. For I have given unto them the words which thou gavest me; and they have received them, and have known surely that I came out from thee, and they have believed that thou didst send me." Jesus said in effect, "Father, everything you told me, I passed on to them."

3. Matthew 13:10-11—"The disciples came, and said unto him, Why speakest thou unto them in parables? He answered and said unto them, Because it is given unto you to know the mysteries of the kingdom of heaven, but to them it is not given." The Lord discloses the nature of God's kingdom to His friends.

4. Luke 10:23-24—Christ "turned unto his disciples, and said privately, Blessed are the eyes which see the things that ye see. For I tell you that many prophets and kings have desired to see those things which ye see, and have not seen them; and to hear those things which ye hear; and have not heard them." For those who are the friends of Jesus, there is an intimacy of knowledge that came from the Father through the Son to us.

5. Acts 20:27—Divine truth first came to the apostles and their companions and was passed on to us through the Word of God. Paul told the Ephesian elders, "I have not shunned to declare unto you all the counsel of God." God's will has been revealed to us in the Bible.

6. Ephesians 3:3-4—Paul said, "By revelation [God] made known unto me the mystery (as I wrote before in few words, by which, when ye read, ye may understand my knowledge in the mystery of Christ)."

7. Romans 16:25-26—"[The] gospel, and the preaching of Jesus Christ, according to the revelation of the mystery . . . was kept secret since the world began, but now is made manifest, and by the scriptures of the prophets, according to the commandment of the everlasting God, made known to all nations for the obedience of faith." God's truth has been revealed to us through the Bible.

8. 1 Corinthians 2:14—Not everyone who reads the Bible can discover its truths, however. Paul tells us that "the natural man receiveth not [does not understand] the things of the Spirit of God; for they are foolishness unto him, neither can he know them, because they are spiritually discerned." The friends of Jesus can know divine truth by the indwelling Spirit and the Word of God. We know things that unbelievers are incapable of understanding. Unbelieving philosophers and scientists are like babes in the wood compared to the simplest Christian who is exposed to the revelation of God through the Word and the ministry of the Holy Spirit. Sometimes we take our privilege of knowing divine truth for granted. I don't think we fully grasp what it is to know the truths of God.

Jesus never expected His disciples to blindly obey Him. We are friends who are intimately acquainted with His heart's desires and the goals of His ministry. What a privilege that is for us who are His disciples today.

III. FRIENDS OF JESUS ARE SPECIALLY CHOSEN (v. 16a-b)

Friends usually choose each other, but Jesus initiates His friendships. Verse 16 says, "Ye have not chosen me, but I have chosen you, and ordained you, that ye should go."

A. Chosen to Salvation (v. 16a)

"Ye have not chosen me, but I have chosen you."

Jesus is talking about salvation here. In verse 19 He says, "I have chosen you out of the world." The Bible teaches that God has sovereignly chosen those who become saved.

1. Ephesians 1:4—"[God] hath chosen us in [Christ] before the foundation of the world."

2. Mark 13:20—Speaking of the Tribulation, Jesus explained, "Except the Lord had shortened those days, no flesh should be saved; but for the elect's sake, whom he hath chosen, he hath shortened the days."

B. Ordained to Service (v. 16b)

"[I have] ordained you, that ye should go."

1. The Explanation

The Greek word translated "ordained" (*tithēmi*) is different from the word translated "chosen." It means "to appoint for special service" or "to send for a special reason." In several places the New Testament talks about certain individuals being appointed or ordained.

a) Luke 6:13-14—"When it was day, [Jesus] called unto him his disciples; and of them he chose twelve." We know that Jesus chose eleven of them to salvation. Beyond that, He chose them to serve as His particular disciples.

b) 1 Corinthians 12:28—Paul delineates those ordained to lead the church: "God hath set some in the church: first apostles, second prophets, third teachers."

c) 2 Timothy 1:11—Paul said, "I am appointed a preacher, and an apostle, and a teacher of the Gentiles." Paul was chosen for certain purposes. Ordination implies service.

2. The Exhortation

a) Stated

There's a difference between being chosen to salvation and being ordained to special service. Verse 16 says that Jesus' friends are ordained to go. No Christian was ever chosen to stand around and watch. We were chosen to go and tell the world about Christ. The world isn't about to come to Christ by itself; we have to go to it. The Bible doesn't say, "Hey, all you in the world, come to church!"

b) Supported

    (1) Luke 14:23—"The lord said unto the servant, Go out into the highways and hedges, and compel them to come in."

    (2) Mark 16:15—Jesus said to His disciples, "Go ye into all the world, and preach the gospel to every creature."

    (3) Acts 1:8—After His resurrection, Jesus told His followers, "Ye shall receive power, after the Holy Spirit is come upon you; and ye shall be witnesses unto me both in Jerusalem, and in Judaea, and in Samaria, and unto the uttermost part of the earth." Christians have been chosen to go out and reach the world. Christ selected a group of men out of the world of darkness, trained them, loved them as friends, and ordained them to go right back into the world where He found them. What a high calling! Every believer has been chosen for salvation and ordained to special service to be fired right back into the world again to communicate Jesus Christ.

    (4) 2 Thessalonians 1:11-12—Paul said, "We pray always for you, that our God would count you worthy of this calling, and fulfill all the good pleasure of his goodness, and the work of faith with power, that the name of our Lord Jesus Christ may be glorified in you." Christians have been called and ordained to glorify the name of Jesus Christ in the world by letting God work His perfect will through them. We're not called to sit; we're called to go.

IV. FRIENDS OF JESUS BEAR FRUIT (v. 16c)

"Bring forth fruit, and that your fruit should remain."

One of the fantastic things about the Christian life is that it's so meaningful. When you go out and communicate the gospel of Jesus Christ to someone who ends up receiving Him, you have brought about an eternal transaction. The life of an unbeliever has only a limited effect on others. It cannot compare with the life of a believer, who bears fruit that is eternal. Like the ripples in a pond when a rock is thrown in, your life will ripple throughout all eternity with fruit born in time to the glory of God.

We have seen that fruit is being Christlike, praising God, contributing to those in need, communicating spiritual truth, doing good works, and leading others to Christ. Those kinds of fruit have eternal consequences in the lives of others. You may say, "But I don't have any eternal fruit—I've never led anyone to Jesus." Maybe you never experienced the final result of reaping the harvest, but the Spirit-produced love and joy in your life can be part of the process of planting the truth of God in others. Even believers you helped lead to Christ in some small way can partly be considered your fruit. Or, when you've taught others the Word of God and enriched their lives, enabling them to better glorify God, you have produced eternal fruit.

It's wonderful to have a life that has such lasting effects. I hope you recognize the significance of your life in Christ—you affect eternity. A true branch doesn't produce temporary fruit but abiding fruit. In 2 Corinthians 5:17 Paul explains the transformation that sharing the gospel can bring about: "If any man be in Christ, he is a new creation; old things are passed away; behold, all things are become new." Paul was in the ministry because he had such a tremendous joy in seeing the finished product and knowing it was eternal. The things you do for God never pass away. Only what's done for Christ will last. The fruit you bear through Him lasts forever. The book of Revelation tells us that believers who have died and gone to heaven will be followed by their works (14:13).

V. FRIENDS OF JESUS HAVE THEIR PRAYERS ANSWERED
(v. 16d)

"That whatever ye shall ask of the Father in my name, he may give it you."

A true friend of Jesus has his prayers answered. To pray in Christ's name simply means to ask for what Jesus would want accomplished. The intent of such praying is not to ask for something so you can "consume it upon your lusts" (James 4:3). When your prayers are aligned with the desires of Jesus Christ, God will answer them.

Conclusion

Those who are the friends of Jesus love each other, know divine truth, have a special calling to go back into the world they've been called out of, bear fruit that is eternal, and have their prayers answered as they pray in the name of Christ. Those are characteristics of all who know Christ. They are yours because of your position in Christ, yet the New Testament still encourages you to operate on those principles. The true friends of Jesus love each other, and yet the Bible says that we must love each other fervently (1 Pet. 4:8). The true friends of Jesus know divine truth, yet the Bible says you should study the Word of God to show yourself "approved unto God . . . rightly dividing the word of truth" (2 Tim. 2:15). The friends of Jesus have been chosen by Him, and yet we are exhorted to "walk worthy" of such a high calling (Eph. 4:1). The friends of Jesus bear eternal fruit, and yet the Bible tells us that we bear "more fruit" as a result of the purging process of the Father (John 15:2). The friends of Jesus pray and God answers, and yet the Bible says we are to pray effectively (James 5:16) and constantly (1 Thess. 5:17). In every one of those general patterns for a Christian, there is also the call for practical implementation to reach for the ideal. The resources are yours if you are a friend of Jesus.

What about those who are not His friends? Jesus said: "He that is not with me is against me" (Matt. 12:30). Are you searching for love and truth? Are you longing for a meaningful, productive life? Are you searching for supernatural resources for all your needs? Be a friend of Jesus, and you'll have them all. Jesus chooses His friends, and if He is calling you to Himself, you need to respond.

Focusing on the Facts

1. How did Jesus comfort the sorrowful disciples before His departure (see p. 55)?
2. What are some of the terms that Scripture uses to identify the believer? In general, what do those terms picture (see p. 55)?
3. What unique intimacy did Jesus bestow on New Testament believers (see pp. 55-56)?
4. What is the condition of friendship with Jesus that is given in John 15:14 (see p. 56)?
5. Can you become a child of God by obedience? Explain (see p. 56).
6. Cite some Scriptures to show that Christians will love other believers (see pp. 57-58).
7. How can the problem of a Christian not loving others be resolved (see p. 58)?
8. What kind of love does Jesus ask us to express (see pp. 58-59)?
9. What do we show the world by exercising sacrificial love (John 13:35; see p. 59)?
10. Cite a verse that identifies believers as beneficiaries of Christ's substitutionary death (see pp. 59-60).
11. Compare the love of God with the love of man (Rom. 5:7-8; see p. 60).
12. How is a Christian's knowledge of his Master's will different from a slave's knowledge of his master's will (see p. 61)?
13. How has divine truth been given to believers? Can an unbeliever understand divine truth? Explain your answer (1 Cor. 2:14; see p. 63).
14. What has God sovereignly chosen some individuals for? What has He ordained those believers to do? Support your answer with Scripture (see pp. 63-64).
15. What type of transaction takes place when we lead someone to Christ (see p. 66)?
16. Why did Paul experience tremendous joy in his ministry (see p. 66)?
17. When can our prayers be answered (see pp. 66-67)?
18. Explain the practical implementation of the ideal of loving others, knowing the truth, sharing Christ, bearing fruit, and

praying according to God's will (see p. 67).

19. According to Matthew 12:30, what is the status of the person who chooses not to be a friend of Jesus but to remain neutral (see p. 67)?

Pondering the Principles

1. Sacrificial love is important to the Christian's testimony. Jesus told His disciples, "By this shall all men know that ye are my disciples, if ye have love one to another" (John 13:35). You have probably heard many sermons encouraging you to love other Christians. But have you ever translated your knowledge into action? Are you loving believers any more now than you were in the past? Are you trying to imitate the sacrificial nature of Christ's love? Or is your love limited to a smile and a handshake and merely being a pleasant person? It's hard to make sacrifices out of love when you are preoccupied with personal comfort and convenience. But Jesus said that the person with the greatest kind of love is willing to sacrifice his life. How great is your love?

2. Sometimes Christians take for granted the privilege of knowing divine truth. As a Christian, do you know where you came from, why you're here, and where you're headed? Are you consistently seeking to better understand the truth that has already been revealed? What are you doing with the truth you do understand? Do you put it into practice and share it with others that their lives may be transformed? Meditate on 1 Corinthians 2, praising God that you have "the mind of Christ" (v. 16).

3. Are you a spectator or a servant? Are you still in the spiritual battle that rages about all true believers? Christ has ordained us that we should serve Him in whatever capacity He has enable us to serve (1 Pet. 4:10-11). Just being on the winning team is exciting, but there is a special joy reserved for the active participants. If you know what your spiritual gifts are, are you involved in ministries that are using them? Are you serving Christ as His ambassador to unbelievers (2 Cor. 5:20)? If you serve Christ faithfully, you will be able to expect the Lord to say, "Well done . . . good and faithful servant" (Matt. 25:21).

5

Hated Without a Cause—Part 1

Outline

Introduction (v. 17)

Lesson
I. Christians Are Not of the World (vv. 18-19)
  A. The Rejection of the World
    1. Explained
    2. Expressed
      a) John 7:7
      b) John 8:23
  B. The Ruler of the World
    1. His purposes
    2. His persecution
      a) 1 John 3:12
      b) John 17:12-15
  C. The Responsibility to the World
    1. Philippians 2:15
    2. 1 John 5:19
    3. Ephesians 5:11
  D. The Reaction of the World
    1. Toward Christ
      a) John 5:16
      b) John 8:58-59
      c) John 10:30-33
    2. Toward its own
    3. Toward Christians
      a) Explained
      b) Expected
      c) Exemplified

Introduction

The end of the fifteenth chapter of John deals with the antagonism of the world toward Jesus and His disciples. In the previous chapters, Jesus has shown that He deeply loves them. Now He shows them the contrast to that love by explaining that the world is going to hate them. This balanced view is designed to eliminate a false expectation of bliss by giving them a realistic understanding of how the world responds to believers.

In verse 17, Jesus makes a transition from describing His love for them to describing the world's hate by saying, "These things I command you, that ye love one another." He is encouraging them to love each other sacrificially and devotedly, just as He has loved them, because they would need each other desperately. The love they had for each other would be all the love they would know, because the world was going to hate them with a passion. The statements beginning in verse 18 are not only a warning about the world's hate but also a motivation for the disciples to love each other.

It's a lonely world for some Christians because other Christians have not always been diligent to express the kind of love for other believers that Jesus Christ wants them to express. The world can be a lonely place because it doesn't accept believers. If we're true disciples of Christ, we run cross-grained to almost everything the world stands for. Consequently, the only love we have to count on and live for is the love of our Savior and fellow believers. So Jesus says to His disciples, 'Men, it's going to be rough. Be sure you keep on loving each other. You desperately need each other in this hostile world."

Christians are encouraged to fervently love their brothers and sisters in Christ (1 Pet. 1:22; 2:17; 4:8). Love is the basis of our relationships within the Body of Christ. We need to love each other as we minister to one another and witness to a hostile world.

Jesus introduces the subject of the world's hatred in contrast to His love and gives four reasons for the hatred of the world.

Lesson

I. CHRISTIANS ARE NOT OF THE WORLD (vv. 18-19)

"If the world hate you, ye know that it hated me before it hated you. If ye were of the world, the world would love its own; but because ye are not of the world, but I have chosen you out of the world, therefore the world hateth you."

A. The Rejection of the World

1. Explained

In this passage, Jesus anticipates that when the disciples move out into the world they're going to experience the hatred of antagonistic unbelievers. He tells them not to be surprised about that because it isn't any different from unbelievers' attitude toward Him. If they are going to stand up for Christ as His followers, they should expect the same kind of treatment.

The world hates believers because they aren't a part of its system. The term *world* (Gk., *kosmos*) is repeatedly used by John. Although it has various meanings, depending on the context, it is used in John 15 to refer to the evil system of sin as it is authored by Satan and acted out by men. It is the expression of human depravity, the instinctual passion for sin that men have. That system of evil is controlled by Satan and his evil angels. Its society of wicked men have set themselves against Christ, His kingdom, and His people. Those who follow and love Jesus Christ—those who openly declare their faith and identify with Christ by what they say and how they live—will be hated by the world because the world has set itself in opposition to everything that is Christlike.

2. Expressed

a) John 7:7—Jesus said this to His earthly brothers, who didn't yet believe in Him: "The world cannot hate you; but me it hateth, because I testify of it, that its works are evil." Jesus was saying, "The world can't hate you because you belong to it. But it hates Me because I confront it with its sin."

b) John 8:23—Jesus said to the Pharisees, "Ye are from beneath; I am from above: ye are of this world; I am not of this world." Jesus implied that those of this world are influenced by the kingdom of hell.

B. The Ruler of the World

1. His purposes

People living in our world who don't know Jesus Christ are part of a satanic system of evil that operates against God. Referring to His coming defeat of Satan at the cross, Jesus said, "Now is the judgment of this world; now shall the prince of this world be cast out" (John 12:31; cf. John 14:30). Satan runs the world's evil system. Naturally Satan's purpose for all that he does is to fight against Christ and God. Therefore his system reflects his evil purposes.

2. His persecution

It's amazing how many Christians are fooled into thinking that the world is tolerant of God and of Jesus Christ when in fact it isn't. The world's many superficial religions are the most heinous and deceptive strategies of Satan. In fact, false religion under the guise of godliness has been the greatest persecutor of the truth throughout church history. Naturally, a society of evil men guided by Satan and his demons and set against God and Christ is going to hate those who belong to Jesus Christ. We need to expect that. If the world doesn't hate you, than maybe you don't belong to Jesus Christ or maybe you aren't living as a Christian should.

a) 1 John 3:12—"Cain, who was of that wicked one . . . killed his brother. And why killed he him? Because his own works were evil, and his brother's righteous." That's why the world hates the true believer—Christians are a condemnation to their evil works. As Cain was indicted by the righteousness of

Abel, so the world is indicted by our righteousness as we stand apart from it. We who have been declared holy in Jesus Christ don't belong to the world's evil system. Therefore the world hates us. Its wicked ruler directs his attack against whomever belongs to God.

b) John 17:12-15—Praying to the Father, Jesus said, "While I was with them in the world, I kept them in thy name; those that thou gavest me I have kept, and none of them is lost. . . . I have given them thy word; and the world hath hated them, because they are not of the world, even as I am not of the world. I pray not that thou shouldest take them out of the world, but that thou shouldest keep them from the evil [one]." Jesus prayed that the Father would protect the disciples from Satan, knowing that his evil system would hate them just as it hated Him. The system hated Jesus Christ so much that its mounting hate finally mocked Him and nailed Him to a cross. Many unbelievers hated Him because He violated their religious system. The greatest persecutors of Christianity have always been false religions and cults—even though they often operate under the guise of godliness. Satan concentrates his efforts toward false religion because that's what captivates people's minds.

C. The Responsibility to the World

God has called Christians to live apart from the system and stand for Jesus Christ.

1. Philippians 2:15—"Be blameless and harmless, children of God, without rebuke, in the midst of a crooked and perverse nation, among whom ye shine as lights in the world." Paul was encouraging the Philippians, who were living in the midst of the godless Roman empire, to have blameless lives that would serve as a rebuke to its corruption.

2. 1 John 5:19—Here the apostle John contrasted believers with the world: "We know that we are of God, and the whole world lieth in wickedness." There is an absolute antithesis between the believer and the world.

3. Ephesians 5:11—Paul said, "Have no fellowship with the unfruitful works of darkness but, rather, reprove them." The believer has the privilege, right, and duty to condemn sin. Perhaps the reason we don't feel as much of the hatred of the world as should be expected is that we aren't willing to confront the world by calling sin what it is. We're far too tolerant and easygoing. We need to confront the unbeliever face-to-face with his sinfulness. The believer who does that will be hated by the world because he openly violates the system and stands in open condemnation of it.

D. The Reaction of the World

1. Toward Christ

Jesus often experienced the hatred of the world when He confronted it.

a) John 5:16—"Therefore did the Jews persecute Jesus, and sought to slay him, because he had done these things on the sabbath day." Jesus violated the Jewish religious system of the day. If you expose a system as false, you will probably get a dramatic reaction. People hate to admit that they are not following the truth but have mistakenly place their lives in something that is wrong. However, if a person does not adhere to a religion, he probably won't have much to be against. But false religion has always been an antagonist of truth.

b) John 8:58-59—Jesus said to the Pharisees, "Verily, verily, I say unto you, Before Abraham was, I am. Then took they up stones to cast at him." Jesus violated their religious system.

c) John 10:30-33—Jesus said to the Pharisees, "I and my Father are one. Then the Jews took up stones again to stone him. Jesus answered them, Many good works have I shown you from my Father; for which of those works do ye stone me? The Jews answered him, saying, For a good work we stone thee not, but for blasphemy; and because that thou, being a man, makest thyself God." People of the world can't tolerate someone who sets himself higher than they are. When you tell someone, "You're living in sin, and you're going to die without God unless you repent and believe the truth," you may get a hostile reaction.

2. Toward its own

The world loves its own. In verse 19 Jesus tells the disciples, "If ye were of the world, the world would love its own." The world finds its unity among the lowest common denominators: It revolves around such things as drinking, carousing, immorality, lying, and cheating.

The more wicked people are, the better the world likes it. Romans 1:32 says that those who have rejected God, although knowing that "they who commit such [evil] things are worthy of death, not only do the same but have pleasure in them that do them." The world glories in its wickedness. It boasts of its unrighteous deeds as if they were significant accomplishments. The world applauds wretched people because it has few moral standards for acceptance. However, when Christians confront the world with a righteous standard that exposes its wretchedness, the world refuses to listen. In fact, the wickedness of the world will only get worse because the world has no conscience. Christians are its conscience. So when we leave the world at the rapture before the Tribulation, all hell will literally break loose because the conscience of the world will be gone.

Revival—Come and Get Condemned!

Christians have been called to be separate from the system and indict it. That's why we can't sit in our lovely churches and say, "I'm certainly praying that the unsaved will come." Let's face it: The world doesn't want to come to church to get indicted by us. Jesus didn't tell us to put up a sign outside that says, "Revival—All unsaved please come Monday through Friday and get condemned"! Rather, we must meet the people of the world outside the church on their own ground. In Matthew 5:13-16 Jesus says, "Ye are the salt of the earth, but if the salt have lost its savor, with

77

what shall it be salted? It is thereafter good for nothing, but to be cast out, and to be trodden under foot of men. Ye are the light of the world. A city that is set on an hill cannot be hidden. Neither do men light a lamp, and put it under a bushel, but on a lampstand. . . . Let your light so shine before men, that they may see your good works, and glorify your Father, who is in heaven." Display your life-style out on a hill, where it belongs, so the world can see it!

3. Toward Christians

a) Explained

Christians are different because Jesus has chosen them "out of the world" (John 15:19). The verb translated "chosen" in that verse appears in the middle (reflexive) voice in Greek and implies that Jesus chose His disciples for Himself. As Christ's own, we stand in direct opposition to Satan's system because our entire manner of life is a living accusation against it. I am sure that infuriates the devil because he doesn't want any defectors from his kingdom. Consequently, he sets out to persecute us through his evil system. Satan hates the righteous as much as he hates God because they identify with the One whose power he is attempting to usurp.

b) Expected

If you really live for Jesus Christ, you will face the antagonism of the world. You can expect that because Jesus experienced it too. In 2 Timothy 3:12 Paul says to Timothy, "All that will live godly in Christ Jesus shall suffer persecution." Generally, the world is going to hate Christians unless it doesn't know certain individuals are believers.

The early Christians were confronting the depravity of the system in their day, which was inundated with false religion. Following their example, if you know someone who's in a cult, you need to tell him in love what he is really involved in. You don't help anyone by being tolerant of sin or of false religious systems.

Knowing that the Jewish religionists were Jesus' greatest antagonists, expect people to hate being told that they have been wrong. The world hates the truth; they never want to be confronted with it, especially by people who claim to be chosen by God. Commentator Arthur Pink says that the one doctrine the world hates most is the doctrine of the sovereignty of God. They refuse to believe that God has chosen Christians to be a part of the true religion (*Exposition of the Gospel of John* [Grand Rapids: Zondervan, 1980], 3:29-30).

c) Exemplified

One of Jesus' most devastating indictments of Israel is found in Luke 4:25-30. When Jesus confronted the Jewish religious leaders with the truth of who He was and stated that they would not accept Him, their hostility erupted. Jesus was the most narrow-minded person who ever lived. Everything He said was absolutely true; anything that ever contradicted what He said was always wrong. In this particular passage, the people of Nazareth were stunned because Jesus, who grew up among them, seemed to know everything. Knowing of their disbelief, Jesus continued to explain how God had sovereignly designed to save Gentiles and temporarily blind Israel: "I tell you of a truth, many widows were in Israel in the days of Elijah, when the heaven was shut up three years and six months, when great famine was throughout all the land; but unto none of them was Elijah sent, but only unto Zarephath, a city of Sidon, unto a woman that was a widow" (vv. 25-26). God can do anything He wants to do. Although there were many widows in Israel, Elijah was sent to help a foreign widow. Being a part of Israel, recipient of the Abrahamic covenant, didn't guarantee divine blessing for every Israelite. Verses 27-30 say, "And many lepers were in Israel in the time of Elisha, the prophet; and none of them was cleansed, but only Naaman, the Syrian. And all they in the synagogue, when they heard these things, were filled with wrath, and rose up, and thrust him out of the city, and led him unto the brow of the hill on which their city was built, that they might cast him down headlong. But he, passing through the midst of them, went his way."

The world hates the sovereignty of God. The fact that Christians have been chosen out of the world and blessed by God doesn't set well with worldly people. They can't understand how non-believing people in a non-Christian nation who haven't heard about Christ can be held accountable by Him. They don't understand about the loving selection of believers by God and that all men are responsible for how they respond to Him because God has revealed Himself to everyone (Rom. 1:18-20). Therefore, expect the world to hate us. If we live godly lives, we're going to be persecuted because we are not of the world—we don't lower ourselves to its standards.

Focusing on the Facts

1. Why did Jesus give His disciples a balanced view of His love and the world's hate (see p. 72)?
2. Why did Jesus encourage His disciples to keep on loving each other sacrificially (see p. 72)?
3. Why are some Christians so lonely in this world (see p. 72)?
4. We Christians need to love each other as we _____ to one another and _____ to a hostile world (see p. 72).
5. Why should Christians not be surprised when they experience the hatred of antagonistic unbelievers (see p. 73)?
6. In the context of John 15, what does *world* refer to (see p. 73)?
7. According to John 7:7, why was Jesus unpopular with the world (see pp. 73-74)?
8. Who rules the world's evil system? What is his purpose in doing so (see p. 74)?
9. What has been the greatest persecutor of truth throughout history (see p. 74)?
10. What did the world's mounting hatred for Jesus finally do (see p. 75)?
11. What responsibility do Christians have with regard to the world? Support your answer with Scripture (see pp. 75-76).
12. Why did the Jewish leaders try to stone Jesus in John 10:30-33 (see p. 76)?
13. According to John 15:19, how does the world respond toward its own? Where does the world find its unity (see p. 77)?

14. If you live for Jesus Christ, standing in direct opposition to Satan's system, what can you expect to face? Support your answer with Scripture (see p. 78).
15. What is one doctrine of God's character that the world especially hates (see pp. 78-79)?
16. Why are all men responsible for how they respond to God (Rom. 1:18-20; see pp. 79-80)?

Pondering the Principles

1. Ephesians 5:11 says, "Do not participate in the unfruitful deeds of darkness, but instead even expose them" (NASB). As a Christian who has been especially chosen by Christ, are you consistently living by His righteous standards? If you have participated in "the unfruitful deeds of darkness," ask God for forgiveness and the power and wisdom to resist further temptations. Maybe you have avoided participating in such deeds, but have you gone a step further and exposed them as you have encountered them? As you confront the world, you will need to do so in a spirit of love and humility. Meditate on 2 Timothy 2:24-26.

2. Are you a closet Christian? Is your life making the impact God designed for it to make on the world? Have you become like salt that has become worthless or a lamp that has been placed under a bushel (Matt. 5:13-15)? You may recall an eagerness to tell the world about Christ when you were first saved, but that has since subsided. Possibly the world has squeezed you into its mold of indifference to spiritual things, or maybe it has silenced you to avoid experiencing its persecution. Don't feel intimidated. Take a stand for Christ, for the gospel is "the power of God unto salvation to everyone that believeth" (Rom. 1:16). The temporary persecution you may endure now will be far outweighed by the joy you will experience from leading those stumbling around in a dark world to "the light of the world" (John 9:5). Pray that God would give you some opportunities to speak of Christ this week, and that He would give you the boldness to speak the truth in love without being worried about the reactions you may encounter.

6

Hated Without a Cause—Part 2

Outline

Introduction

Review
I. Christians Are Not of the World (vv. 18-19)
   A. The Rejection of the World
   B. The Ruler of the World
   C. The Responsibility to the World
   D. The Reaction of the World

Lesson
II. The World Hated Jesus (v. 20)
   A. The Principle of Identification (v. 20*a*)
      1. Explained
      2. Exemplified
         a) Philippians 3:10
         b) Galatians 6:17
      3. Exhorted
   B. The Promise of Persecution (v. 20*b*)
      1. Explained
      2. Exemplified
III. The World Doesn't Know God (vv. 21-25)
   A. Explaining the Reason (v. 21)
      1. 1 Corinthians 10:20
      2. Acts 17:22-23
      3. 1 Corinthians 2:7-8

B. Examining Its Rejection (vv. 22-24)
  1. Of Jesus' words (v. 22)
     a) Explained
     b) Expressed
     c) Exemplified
  2. Of Jesus' Father (v. 23)
  3. Of Jesus' works (v. 24)
C. Exposing Its Responsibility (v. 25)

Conclusion

Introduction

In Acts 1:8, as Jesus Christ is preparing to ascend into heaven, He tells His disciples, "Ye shall receive power, after the Holy Spirit is come upon you; and ye shall be witnesses unto me both in Jerusalem, and in all Judaea, and in Samaria, and unto the uttermost part of the earth." The Greek word for "witnesses" is *marturēs*, from which the English word "martyr" is derived. A martyr came to refer to someone who died for a cause, because witnesses for Jesus Christ often lost their lives as a result of their unwavering Christian testimony.

Knowing that persecution would come, Jesus warns His disciples in John 15 to balance out the wonderful promises He has given them. He said they would have unlimited power to do even greater things than He had done when He was present (John 14:12). He said they would have peace (John 14:27) and joy (John 15:11) and that they would lack nothing (John 15:7). Such blessings would give them the ability to confront the world with truth. In John 15:26-27 Jesus promises the disciples, "When the Comforter is come, whom I will send unto you from the Father, even the Spirit of truth, who proceedeth from the Father, he shall testify of me; and ye also shall bear witness, because ye have been with me from the beginning." He told them that their witnessing would be energized by the Holy Spirit. But to keep them from thinking that because of the promises and power available to them they wouldn't encounter negative reactions, Jesus told them that the world would hate and persecute them for their testimony. In fact, He said, the world, which is steeped in false religion, would think it was serving God by killing them (John 16:1-2).

Review

On the last night before His crucifixion, Jesus not only gave His disciples promises that would become reality in His absence, but He also gave them a warning to be aware of the world's hatred. Those who are Christ's—those who are willing to deny themselves, take up their cross, and follow Him daily—will be hated for three reasons.

I. CHRISTIANS ARE NOT OF THE WORLD (vv. 18-19; see pp. 73-80)

   A. The Rejection of the World (see pp. 73-74)

   The world hates Christians because they are not of this world's evil system, which is controlled by Satan and his evil angels. The world is a society of wicked men who have set themselves against God and His kingdom. Because the heart of the system is false religion, whether atheistic humanism, idolatry, cults, or theological liberalism, the world hates those who belong to the true religion. Don't be surprised that the world hates you, because it hated Christ. The world loves only "its own" (v. 19). It is not that the people of the world actually love one another; it is that each individual in the world loves himself and his possessions. He loves others only insofar as loving others will bring advantage to himself. The love of the world is selfish and superficial. Naturally the world would not love Christians because they confront and condemn it by their pure lives and the Word of God.

   B. The Ruler of the World (see pp. 74-75)

   First John 5:19 implies that the whole world lies in Satan's lap. The people of the world are not unhappy under his rule; they're naively content with it. The world is self-satisfied and complacent, indifferent to God and unaware of its lostness. It has been lulled by Satan into doubting God's judgment. Consequently, when you and I come along and try to wake it up with disturbing messages of sin and judgment, the world responds with hated toward the message and the messengers. Verse 18 says, "If the world hate you, ye know that it hated me before it hated you." In the Greek

85

text, verse 18 is a first-class condition, which emphasizes the reality of the statement: We can be sure that the world hates those who are visibly committed to Christ.

Every man is born into this world as a part of Satan's system. Whether he likes it or not, he is under the headship of Satan, who is "the god of this world" (2 Cor. 4:4, KJV). Ephesians 2:1-2 says that when we were "dead in trespasses and sins," we walked "according to the course of this world, according to the prince of the power of the air." The unsaved individual has a Satan-centered existence. However when a person acknowledges Christ as Lord by faith, that's a sign that he's been chosen "out of the world" (John 15:19). In Colossians 1:13, Paul says that God "hath delivered us from the power of darkness, and hath translated us into the kingdom of his dear Son."

C. The Responsibility to the World (see pp. 75-76)

The world hates us because of the liberty that is ours in Christ, which brings with it newfound joy, confidence, and a sense of belonging to an eternal kingdom. The fact that we know the truth and confront the world's sin brings about jealous antagonism.

D. The Reaction of the World (see pp. 76-80)

If we walk worthy of our calling, the world will hate us. Timothy perhaps needed to share that with the people to whom he was ministering, so Paul tells him in 2 Timothy 3:11-12, "Persecutions, afflictions, which came unto me at Antioch, at Iconium, at Lystra, what persecutions I endured; but out of them all the Lord delivered me. Yea, and all that will live godly in Christ Jesus shall suffer persecution." If there isn't any antagonism in the world toward you, then perhaps you don't have a visible, Christlike testimony.

II. THE WORLD HATED JESUS (v. 20)

A. The Principle of Identification (v. 20*a*)

"Remember the word that I said unto you, The servant is not greater than his lord."

1. Explained

The world hates us because they hated Jesus Christ, whom we represent. Hate isn't something that can be stored up for very long; it has to be vented. The world has always hated Christ and now that He is gone, they unleash their hatred on those who represent Him. We get the brunt of the hatred that is ultimately directed toward Christ. Let me assure you that the hatred of the world is just as real today as it was two thousand years ago. There are people all over the world dying for their faith in Jesus Christ.

In chapter 13, Jesus uses the principle of a servant's not being greater than his lord in talking about service. He was telling His disciples, "I'm concerned that you humbly wash each other's feet as I have done to you, and serve one another." But in chapter 15, He's using the same principle to apply to persecution, saying, "You don't think that if your Master is persecuted that you're going to get away without persecution, do you?"

2. Exemplified

a) Philippians 3:10—Paul talked about "the fellowship of [Christ's] sufferings." He knew firsthand what sharing and identifying with the sufferings of Christ meant.

b) Galatians 6:17—You may have collected some trophies for past accomplishments. The apostle Paul had a very interesting trophy case: his body. He said, "I bear in my body the marks of the Lord Jesus." I can imagine when someone had a chance to see his back he might wonder where Paul received all his scars. Paul might have said, "Do you see those stripes across the back? I got those for the sake of Jesus." I believe he loved every one of them, because he could say, "For to me to live is Christ, and to die is gain" (Phil. 1:21). He counted the things he had previously valued before becoming a Christian as refuse in his striving to become more like Christ (Phil. 3:8). Paul was a committed disciple who identified with Jesus Christ. He experienced the same kind of abuse that the world gave to Jesus until he himself was martyred. Paul shared in the sufferings of Christ. Most Christians don't have the joy of knowing what it is to suffer the rebuke and hatred of the world for Christ's sake because they fail to identify completely with Him.

3. Exhorted

In 1 Peter 2:21 Peter says, "Christ also suffered for us, leaving us an example, that ye should follow his steps." The word "example" (Gk., *hupogrammon*, "a copy") established a pattern of suffering for Christians to follow in confronting the world. Verse 23-24 explain how He suffered: Jesus, "when he was reviled, reviled not again; when he suffered, he threatened not, but committed himself to him that judgeth righteously." Jesus never retaliated for the suffering He received; He took it willingly. He not only suffered on the cross to take away our sin, but He suffered to give us a pattern of how to confront the world. If the world abuses us, we ought to take it in silence and count ourselves worthy to have suffered like Jesus. Don't be surprised if you suffer; our Lord did, and His servants are not exempt from the same kind of treatment.

B. The Promise of Persecution (v. 20*b*)

"If they have persecuted me, they will also persecute you; if they have kept my saying, they will keep yours also."

1. Explained

Jesus was saying to His disciples, "You're going to have the same situation that I had: Some people are going to persecute you and some people are going to accept your words. There's going to be a vast majority that will be antagonistic toward you. However, there will be some who accept what you say." Most Christians don't experience the persecution that Jesus said would be common because their lives revolve only around church activities. If they tried going door to door announcing that people are sinners in line for the judgment of God in an eternal hell, the reactions would be different than what they are accustomed to. We aren't doing our job of confronting the world if we confine our Christianity to ourselves.

If we follow Christ's example, the unbelieving world is going to persecute us. Although some will accept Christ's teaching and therefore that of His servants, their number will be fewer than the antagonists. In Matthew 7:13-14 Jesus says, "Wide is the gate, and broad is the way, that leadeth to destruction, and many there be who go in that way; because narrow is the gate, and hard is the way, which leadeth unto life, and few there be that find it." I heard a minister say there's going to be more people in heaven than there will be in hell. But I don't believe that for a minute. Only a believing remnant will be there. In spite of that, our responsibility is to confront the world and suffer whatever abuse may come, joyfully knowing that some will hear the gospel and believe.

2. Exemplified

In Acts 7, a man named Stephen becomes one of the first martyrs of the church. After preaching a great gospel message, he indicted the religious leaders for their hardheartedness, saying, "Which of the prophets have not your fathers persecuted? And they have slain them who showed before the coming of the Just One, of whom ye have been now the betrayers and murderers; who have received the law by the disposition of angels, and have not kept it" (vv. 52-53). The religious leaders were furious: "When they heard these things, they were cut to the heart, and they gnashed on him with their teeth. But he, being full of the Holy Spirit, looked up steadfastly into heaven, and saw the glory of God, and Jesus standing on the right hand of God, and said, Behold, I see the heavens opened, and the Son of man standing on the right hand of God. Then they cried out with a loud voice, and stopped their ears, and ran upon him with one accord, and cast him out of the city, and stoned him; and the witnesses laid down their clothes at a young man's feet, whose name was Saul. And they stoned Stephen, calling upon God, and saying, Lord Jesus, receive my spirit. And he kneeled down, and cried with a loud voice, Lord, lay not this sin to their charge. And when he had said this, he fell asleep. And Saul was consenting unto his death. And at that time there was a great persecution against the church which was at Jerusalem; and they were all scattered abroad throughout the regions of Judaea and Samaria, except the apostles. And devout men carried Stephen to his burial, and made great lamentation over him" (Acts 7:54—8:2). That's an example of the world's hatred of those who confront their sin.

When you confront men with their sin, expect a reaction. Sometimes they'll receive Christ, but more times than not they will react violently. If you're not getting a reaction from the world, you're probably not confronting it.

III. THE WORLD DOESN'T KNOW GOD (vv. 21-25)

The hardest fact for the world to swallow is that it doesn't really know God. You can imagine how that fact was received by the religious leaders Jesus presented it to, for they prided themselves on their knowledge of God. But when Jesus repeatedly told them that they really didn't know God, they became greatly infuriated. The inner cause of all hate is the absence of a knowledge of God.

A. Explaining the Reason (v. 21)

"But all these things will they do unto you for my name's sake, because they know not him that sent me."

90

Jesus told His disciples that people were going to persecute and even kill them because of their hatred for Him and their ignorance about God. Man is born into the world as an enemy of God. He is indifferent, rebellious, and hateful toward God. Men don't know God, let alone love Him. But what about religious people? Being religious doesn't mean you know God either.

1. 1 Corinthians 10:20—People in false religions "sacrifice to demons, and not to God." False religion is demoniacally inspired. Advocates of theological liberalism and modernism claim to be Christian, yet deny the virgin birth and deity of Christ and the verbal inspiration of Scripture. They don't love God; they hate Him. They are under Satan's control, whether they are flagrant atheists or superficial liberals. An individual who doesn't worship the true God through Jesus Christ is essentially an atheist, no matter what else he may worship. Worshiping the wrong God is a form of atheism because one is worshiping a god who doesn't exist.

2. Acts 17:22-23—The world does indeed worship a god who doesn't exist. When Paul arrived in Athens, he stood on Mars Hill and said, "Ye men of Athens, I perceive that in all things ye are very religious. For as I passed by, and beheld your devotions, I found an altar with this inscription, TO THE UNKNOWN GOD. Whom, therefore, ye ignorantly worship. . ." The religious Athenians were worshiping a god they didn't even know. That is typical of man's approach to religion. He postulates a god who doesn't exist and then worships it. In spite of that, he is, in effect, an atheist.

3. 1 Corinthians 2:7-8—Paul said, "We speak the wisdom of God in a mystery, even the hidden wisdom, which God ordained before the ages unto our glory; which none of the princes of this age knew; for had they known it, they would not have crucified the Lord of glory." Paul says, "If men had known God, they never would have crucified Jesus Christ." And if men knew God today, they wouldn't continue to crucify "the Son of God afresh, and put him to an open shame" by rejecting the truth (Heb. 6:6). That's proof that they don't know God

at all. If an individual has never invited Jesus Christ into his life and received Him as personal Savior—I don't care who that individual is or what he thinks he knows—he has no knowledge of God at all. No man ever knew God who rejected Jesus Christ, who is God in human flesh. The main reason people hate Christ and Christians is that they don't know God and are lulled by satanic counterfeit religions into thinking that they do. That's why false religion is such a curse. I believe Satan spends most of his time in false religion.

Is Everyone Responsible to Know God?

Someone might say, "It's not my fault I'm ignorant of God. I came into the world not knowing God, so you can't hold me responsible!" Everyone is responsible, however. Romans 1:18-19 says, "The wrath of God is revealed from heaven against all ungodliness and unrighteousness of men, who hold the truth in unrighteousness, because that which may be known of God is manifest in them; for God hath shown it unto them." Every man comes into this world with the basic knowledge that God exists. Not only from his innate knowledge is God revealed but from creation as well. Verse 20 says, "The invisible things of him from the creation of the world are clearly seen, being understood by the things that are made, even his eternal power and Godhead, so that they are without excuse."

But if all the information is there, how did man get to the place of not knowing God? Verses 21-23 tell us: "Because, when they knew God, they glorified him not as God, neither were thankful, but became vain in their imaginations, and their foolish heart was darkened. Professing themselves to be wise, they became fools, and changed the glory of the incorruptible God into an image made like corruptible man." The result of false religion comes in verse 28: "Even as they did not like to retain God in their knowledge, God gave them over to a reprobate [worthless] mind." Men are born as rebels against God but with an innate knowledge that He exists. In John 1:9, Jesus is said to be "the true Light, which lighteth every man." Men know the truth of God, yet they willingly reject God and Christ—not because of ignorance, but because of their wickedness. Men love darkness rather than light (John 3:19). They are like bugs that hide under a rock and scatter when the rock is moved, exposing them to light. Men don't know God because of their own wickedness and rejection of God's full revelation. That is the most serious sin that can be committed.

B. Examining Its Rejection (vv. 22-24)

1. Of Jesus' words (v. 22)

"If I had not come and spoken unto them, they had not had sin; but now they have no cloak for their sin."

a) Explained

That is one of the most important verses in the book of John. Jesus is not talking about sin in general, because whether He came or not, men would still be sinners. Rather, He's talking about the sin of willful rejection in the presence of total revelation. The greatest sin that a man can commit is to have the specifics of God's revelation and then reject it. Jesus is saying, "I have told you the truth and yet you have rejected it. Therefore, the cloak of your hypocrisy is ripped off—you can't hide your sin of willful rejection anymore! It has been made obvious by your spurning Me."

The greatest sin that a man can commit is rejecting God's full revelation. When the world killed Jesus, they did it in the face of full revelation. God had given them the Old Testament and then Christ Himself. They heard what He said and saw what He did, yet they killed Him, reacting to all that God had communicated to man with hatred and unbelief. Jesus is saying, "If I hadn't come and given you full display of revelation, you never could have committed the sin of rejection against full revelation. But now that I have come and have revealed God to you, yet you rejected, you've committed that sin."

b) Expressed

Hebrews 6:4-6, an important and much misunderstood passage, deals with that very sin: "It is impos-

93

sible for those who were once enlightened, and have tasted of the heavenly gift, and were made partakers of the Holy Spirit, and have tasted the good word of God, and the powers of the age to come, if they shall fall away, to renew them again unto repentance, seeing they crucify to themselves the Son of God afresh, and put him to an open shame." When someone has been enlightened with the full revelation of God and has seen what the Spirit of God can do, yet rejects the truth, he can never turn from his rejection. He has made a full rejection in the face of total revelation, and there is therefore no more revelation available for him to receive.

That passage is not talking about a Christian's losing his salvation, because verse 9 makes a contrasting transition into salvation: "But, beloved, we are persuaded better things of you, and things that accompany salvation." The verses prior refer to the man who has full revelation but hasn't responded to it with saving faith. Verses 4-6 merely refer to getting insights into the truth. So when a man receives all the information God has given, yet still rejects it, he has committed a sin for which there's no remedy.

c) Exemplified

Matthew 12 illustrates how a group of people rejected Christ at the point of total revelation and were left with no other recourse for salvation. The Pharisees had seen Jesus' life and His miracles, and they had heard Him speak. God couldn't have given them clearer revelation. Although they were students of the Old Testament and had just seen the Lord cast a demon out of a person, this was their conclusion: "This fellow doth not cast out demons, but by Beelzebub, the prince of the demons" (v. 24). In other words, "He's casting out demons because He's demon possessed." They concluded that Jesus was from hell—the exact opposite of what they should have concluded based on the revelation they had seen and heard. In response, Jesus said, "All manner of sin and blasphemy shall be forgiven men; but the blasphemy against the Holy Spirit shall not be forgiven men.

And whosoever speaketh a word against the Son of man, it shall be forgiven him; but whosoever speaketh against the Holy Spirit, it shall not be forgiven him, neither in this age, neither in the age to come" (vv. 31-32).

What exactly is the blasphemy of the Holy Spirit? Since all Christ did was accomplished through the Spirit, He was saying, "If you have seen all the works that the Holy Spirit has done through Me, yet have concluded they were of Satan, you have blasphemed the Holy Spirit." Blasphemy of the Holy Spirit is attributing the works and words of Christ to Satan. You cannot be forgiven for that. The Jewish religious leaders had total revelation, yet they made a total rejection. Consequently, there was no way they could ever be saved. I don't believe, however, that this "unpardonable sin" can be committed during the church age because Jesus isn't now here on earth making a divine display of His power. But I think it will be committed again in His kingdom after He comes back.

People who appear to be religious and to worship God, yet who do not receive Jesus Christ as Savior have spurned the most complete revelation of God. Such people don't know God at all—they're hypocrites. John 15:22 rips away the cloak of hypocrisy and uncovers their sin.

2. Of Jesus' Father (v. 23)

"He that hateth me hateth my Father also."

That statement is crystal clear: The Pharisees didn't love God. They couldn't love God and hate His Son—that is impossible. They were practical atheists who played a religious game; they didn't know God. Men who mock Jesus don't know God. And men who reduce Jesus to just a good moral teacher don't know or love God either. In John 5:23 Jesus says, "He that honoreth not the Son honoreth not the Father, who hath sent him." Don't ever be deceived into thinking that someone can love God and not Jesus Christ. Some people who reject Christ don't appear as violent haters of God, but Jesus said, "He that is not with me is against me" (Matt. 12:30). Some men persecute the followers of Jesus because they don't know God. But it is inexcusable not to know God, because He has given you full revelation for which you're responsible. Romans 1:20 says that men "are without excuse."

3. Of Jesus' works (v. 24)

"If I had not done among them the works which no other man did, they had not had sin; but now they have both seen and hated both me and my Father."

Jesus was saying, "I've displayed the Father in My works so that they've seen the Father working through Me, yet they've concluded that I'm from hell." People rejected His works as well as His words. I especially can't figure out how they could have rejected His works. They must have known about how He had raised Lazarus from the dead. Imagine the setting in front of the tomb: "Jesus said, Take away the stone. Martha, the sister of him that was dead, saith unto him, Lord, by this time he stinketh; for he hath been dead four days" (John 11:39). She probably thought that even though the odor of a decaying corpse would be awful, Jesus wanted to say a last good-bye to Lazarus. Convincing her to let the stone be rolled away, Jesus said, "Lazarus, come forth" (v. 43). Resurrection is the acid test of divine power. You can go down to the local cemetery and say, "Come out!" until you're purple in the face, but no one's going to come out —except maybe the caretaker. However, when Jesus commanded Lazarus to come out, Scripture says, "He that was dead came forth" (v. 44). The process of decay was reversed, and Lazarus stood up and walked out of the grave.

The Jewish religious leaders knew about that miracle because they saw Lazarus and word about him spread everywhere. But it didn't matter what Jesus did—their hearts were so willfully hardened against Him. They loved their darkness and sin. They loved their pride and willfully said no to Jesus Christ, blaspheming the Holy Spirit. Men still reject Christ. Their hateful rejection of

Christ's words and deeds, which reveal the Father, shows that they hate the Father as well.

C. Exposing Its Responsibility (v. 25)

"But this cometh to pass, that the word might be fulfilled that is written in their law, They hated me without a cause."

That statement is in two of David's psalms. Psalm 35:19 and 69:4 foreshadow the Messiah's being hated "without a cause." Jesus spoke enough words and did enough deeds to make them responsible so that by hating Him, they would be hating Him without a cause. In that way God erased every reason for a man to hate Jesus. If men continue to hate Jesus, they do it for no other reason than their own sin. There's no good reason to hate Jesus. God didn't plan that people should hate Him. But He planned that if they did, they would do so without any good reason. God has given us full revelation so that if a man hates Christ, he does it without any cause at all, except his own sinfulness. Jesus manifested such a pure and attractive revelation of God that if a man hated Him, he would do so without reason. There's nothing in Jesus to make a man hate Him. Doing everything to save men and keep them out of hell, God wanted to make sure that He removed every vestige of excuse, leaving a man only with his own sin as the reason for his hatred.

Conclusion

The world hated Jesus because He exposed their sin. He showed them who they were, and they didn't like it. When Jesus turned the spotlight of His divine holiness on the sins of the people, they writhed and rebelled under it because He stripped away the darkness and laid bare what was in their hearts. However, instead of turning to Him in loving faith and receiving forgiveness and the salvation He offered, they turned against Him.

The world still hates Jesus as well as those who are His and who live for Him and love Him. Therefore, if you're going to count the cost and be a disciple of Jesus Christ, you will find that true discipleship necessitates a willingness to suffer the hatred of the world. And if you're not willing to suffer the hatred of the world, then you're not really willing to be the disciple that Jesus wants you to be. Persecution is a part of true Christianity.

Many of you, perhaps, believe that you've beaten the problem of the world's hatred by being a friend of the world. If you're a friend of the world, then you're no friend of God. First John 2:15 says, "If any man love the world, the love of the Father is not in him." James 4:4 says, "Friendship with the world is hostility toward God" (NASB). If you're wrapped up in the system, you're violating everything that discipleship stands for.

The subtle temptation of Satan is to get us to the point where we don't want to offend anyone. When we do that, we violate everything that Jesus desires in our lives. He didn't send us into the world to make it comfortable; He sent us into the world to make it miserable. Start offending people with the truth for their own good. Start rebuking and start reproving their sin. Paul said, "Have no fellowship with the unfruitful works of darkness but, rather, reprove them" (Eph. 5:11).

We need to preach the offense of the cross. In 1 Corinthians 1:23 Paul says, "We preach Christ crucified, unto the Jews a stumbling block, and unto the Gentiles foolishness." In the next chapter he says, "I determined not to know any thing among you, except Jesus Christ, and him crucified" (v. 2). In Galatians 6:14 he says, "God forbid that I should glory, except in the cross of our Lord Jesus Christ, by whom the world is crucified unto me, and I unto the world." Paul could have dropped the cross from his message. He could have neglected to condemn sin to eliminate the stumbling block and be acceptable in the Greco-Roman and Jewish world. But he wouldn't have been acceptable to God.

Are we living holy lives? Are we confronting sin and calling it what it is? Every Christian needs to confront the world by exposing and reproving sin, whatever the cost. If perhaps you are an unbeliever, you need to recognize that you have no excuse. How you respond to Jesus will seal your eternity.

Focusing on the Facts

1. Why did the word *martyr* become synonymous with death (see p. 84)?
2. What would enable the disciples to confront the world? Support your answer with Scripture (see p. 84).
3. Describe the kind of love that characterizes the world (see p. 85).
4. What system is every man a part of when he is born into the world (see p. 86)?
5. Now that Jesus is not on earth anymore, where is the world's hatred directed (see p. 87)?
6. Explain the principle of a servant not being greater than his lord (John 15:20; see pp. 87-88).
7. Why do most Christians not experience the joy of suffering the rebuke and hatred of the world for Christ's sake (see p. 88)?
8. According to 1 Peter 2:21, what kind of example did Christ leave for believers (see p. 88)?
9. Will those who accept Christ's teaching be fewer or greater in number than those who ultimately reject it? Support your answer with Scripture (see p. 89).
10. What kind of reaction did Stephen get in Acts 7 after he confronted the hardheartedness of the religious leaders (see pp. 89-90)?
11. What is one of the hardest things for the world to accept? Why (see p. 90)?
12. How is it possible for religious people not to know God and even to be considered atheists in a sense (see pp. 91-92)?
13. If men had truly known God, what never would have happened, according to 1 Corinthians 2:7-8 (see pp. 91-92)?
14. Why is false religion such a curse (see p. 92)?
15. Is everyone responsible to know God? Explain (see pp. 92-93).
16. How did man get to the point of not knowing God (Rom. 1:21-23; see p. 92)?
17. What is the greatest sin that a man can commit (see p. 93)?
18. Why is it impossible for someone who understands the truth and rejects it to turn from his rejection and believe in God (Heb. 6:4-6; see pp. 93-94)?
19. What do the Pharisees conclude about Jesus in Matthew 12:24? Why was their sin unpardonable (see pp. 94-95)?
20. Cite a Scripture verse to show that people who mock Jesus or merely consider Him a good moral teacher do not know or love God (see pp. 95-96).

21. What miracle was Christ's greatest demonstration of divine power (see pp. 96)?
22. Since there is no good reason to hate Jesus, what is the only reason left for a person's hating him (see p. 97)?
23. Why did the world hate Jesus (see p. 97)?
24. What does true discipleship necessitate a willingness to do (see pp. 97-98)?
25. Explain why Jesus sent believers into the world (Eph. 5:11; see p. 98).

Pondering the Principles

1. Meditate on 1 Peter 2:18-25. How are Christians supposed to respond to those in authority over them (v. 18)? What if their superiors are unreasonable? What type of response to unjust treatment finds favor with God (vv. 19-20)? What example did Christ leave for us (vv. 21-22)? Rather than retaliating, what did He do (v. 23)? Evaluate your own response to unjust suffering. Are you argumentative, or do you let your anger smolder? The next time you seek to retaliate for something you don't deserve, entrust yourself to "Him who judges righteously" (v. 23, NASB). That doesn't mean you can't appeal to those who have wronged you. It does mean, however, that you put your initial reaction and the ultimate result in the hands of God.

2. Are you living a holy life? Are you confronting sin and calling it what it is? Knowing that Christians will be ridiculed and antagonized for doing those things shouldn't cause us to shirk our responsibility. Many times we compromise our convictions and avoid confronting wrong because we so greatly value the acceptance of others. As you share the truth with those in your sphere of influence, recognize that you aren't responsible for how they respond to the truth. Realize also if you have to make the choice, it is far better to be accepted by the God who redeemed you than by those who hate your Redeemer.

Scripture Index

102